# GOD

## ⋍ IN THE ⋍

# REARVIEW

# MIRROR

**LaVila Henry**

*To Heather from Jim & Wanda Jordan*

*LaVila is like a sister to us! All these stories are her real life — just thought you'd like it. (Jim's story on pg. 47)*

*God's best blessings LaVila Henry Phil 4:13*

**CHP**

GOD IN THE REARVIEW MIRROR:
FINDING HOPE WHEN THE PATH SEEMS DIM
by LaVila Henry
Published by Creation House Press
A Charisma Media Company
600 Rinehart Road
Lake Mary, Florida 32746
www.charismamedia.com

Unless otherwise noted, all Scripture quotations are from the King James Version of the Bible.

Scripture quotations marked ESV are from the Holy Bible, English Standard Version, copyright © 2001 by Crossway Bibles, a division of Good News Publisher. Used by permission.

Scripture quotations marked NIV are from the Holy Bible, New International Version. Copyright © 1973, 1978, 1984, 2010, 2011, International Bible Society. Used by permission.

Scripture quotations marked NLT are from the Holy Bible, New Living Translation, copyright © 1996. Used by permission of Tyndale House Publishers, Inc., Wheaton, IL 60189. All rights reserved.

The names of some friends and family members have been changed to protect the privacy of the individuals involved.

Design Director: Justin Evans
Cover design by Judith McKittrick Wright

Library of Congress Control Number: 2016930249
International Standard Book Number: 978-1-62998-523-7
E-book International Standard Book Number:
978-1-62998-524-4

While the author has made every effort to provide accurate telephone numbers and Internet addresses at the time of publication, neither the publisher nor the author assumes any responsibility for errors or for changes that occur after publication.

First edition

16 17 18 19 20 — 987654321

Printed in the United States of America

*To my husband, Paul. Without your
support I never could have accomplished
this goal. It is just as much your book
as mine—well, almost. I love you.*

# CONTENTS

|                      | Introduction . . . . . . . . . . . . . ix |
| -------------------- | ----------------------------------------- |
| **Chapter One:**     | Kindness Counts . . . . . . . . . 1 |
| **Chapter Two:**     | Son Shine. . . . . . . . . . . . . . . 3 |
| **Chapter Three:**   | Smarter than You Think. . . . 7 |
| **Chapter Four:**    | A Season for Everything. . . 11 |
| **Chapter Five:**    | Discord Strikes . . . . . . . . . . 15 |
| **Chapter Six:**     | Second Chances . . . . . . . . . 19 |
| **Chapter Seven:**   | In-laws or Outlaws . . . . . . . 21 |
| **Chapter Eight:**   | Free at Last . . . . . . . . . . . . . 25 |
| **Chapter Nine:**    | Let the Show Begin . . . . . . . 29 |
| **Chapter Ten:**     | Meeting at the Top . . . . . . . 33 |
| **Chapter Eleven:**  | Caution to the Wind. . . . . . 39 |
| **Chapter Twelve:**  | 911 . . . . . . . . . . . . . . . . . . . . 43 |
| **Chapter Thirteen:** | Sleeping Beauty . . . . . . . . . 47 |
| **Chapter Fourteen:** | Who's Your Mama? . . . . . . . 51 |
| **Chapter Fifteen:** | The Hometown Crowd . . . . 55 |
| **Chapter Sixteen:** | A Lemon Becomes |
|                      | Lemonade . . . . . . . . . . . . . . . 59 |
| **Chapter Seventeen:** | The Big Surprise! . . . . . . . . 65 |
| **Chapter Eighteen:** | Giving a Good Pounding. . . 69 |
| **Chapter Nineteen:** | Degrees of Blessing . . . . . . . 73 |

| | | |
|---|---|---|
| **Chapter Twenty:** | Back to the Future | 77 |
| **Chapter Twenty-One:** | Good Grief, Lady!. | 81 |
| **Chapter Twenty-Two:** | Welcome Home | 85 |
| **Chapter Twenty-Three:** | Let the Decorating Begin. | 89 |
| **Chapter Twenty-Four:** | Rx: The Best | 91 |
| **Chapter Twenty-Five:** | Roots. | 95 |
| **Chapter Twenty-Six:** | The Buck Starts Here | 97 |
| **Chapter Twenty-Seven:** | Alone? | 99 |
| **Chapter Twenty-Eight:** | A Stroke of Genius. | 103 |
| **Chapter Twenty-Nine:** | In Conclusion | 107 |
| | Notes | 111 |
| | About the Author | 113 |
| | Contact the Author | 115 |

# INTRODUCTION

WHEN YOU PUT your own life's experiences out there, you're open for possible criticism. Someone may say, "Well, stupid, you should have known better than that"; or, "You told that story to toot your own horn"; or, "I don't believe a word of it." And, there is always the chance the way each of us remembers things isn't quite the same. However, I've done my very best to be as accurate as possible. And speaking of accuracy brings to remembrance an incident from many years ago.

I had advertised in the newspaper several pair of Paul's dress shoes he was through with. (I know; you're wondering what this has to do with accuracy. You'll get the point by the end.) Anyway, a guy called and made an appointment to see the shoes. I remember looking out the side window by the front door after he rang the doorbell and thinking his feet looked too big for the shoes. When he came in I had a creepy feeling. After looking at the shoes, he asked if he could use the restroom. I didn't want to say, "No, get out!" for fear of what he might do. Thankfully, not far from our front door was a half bath. I pointed him in that direction.

My hand firmly on the front door knob, I was ready to bolt. *If he comes out of there naked or partially clothed,* I thought, *I'm outta here.* He soon reappeared with his clothes intact. Relieved, I opened the door and he left. His license plate wasn't visible from where I was standing, but I tried to remember the details of his car.

The next day at the real estate office where I worked I was telling about my experience. A couple of the guys insisted the details of the car couldn't be right, causing me to doubt some of my description. Overhearing the entire conversation, my friend and colleague, Lillian, informed me the same thing had happened to a woman she knew—a man had answered her ad, didn't buy anything, and asked to use the restroom before he left. That made me curious. I called the *Times Call*, our local newspaper, and reported the incident to them. They thought it was strange, but said they would do nothing. I decided to report it to the police. I was informed they would only get involved if a crime had been committed.

Feeling no release from the situation, I began calling the newspaper ads to see if it had happened to anyone else. It had. There were many with the same scenario and others who hadn't received his visit. I left my name and number with each of them. A few days later the call came. He had just left her house and she had gotten his license plate number. And (here we go!) my recollection of his car had been totally correct. Once again I contacted the police. They weren't willing to share much information; but I did gain the knowledge that the mystery man was known to them, and at that point from all indications his visits to the advertisers stopped.

As amateur sleuths we were in agreement it was highly unlikely he had overactive bladder syndrome that caused his bathroom visits. Several of us decided he may have been casing houses. Visiting the bathroom in most abodes would give you a pretty good view of the entire floor plan. However, it is something we will never know for sure.

I wish I could tell you this story had a wonderful *God in the Rearview Mirror* ending. It doesn't. But here is the point I told you I would make—plus a bonus point.

- Point 1: Unless you're known for your poor memory or someone has concrete evidence to the contrary, don't believe your recollections are wrong just because someone tries to tell you otherwise.

- Point 2: There may be an important ending to your story that you simply never find out.

However, the accounts in this book all have an ending where God allowed us to see Him, at least in part, in the rearview mirror.

I've included life-altering stories as well as those that may seem less dramatic. It is my desire that we not only celebrate the big things God does for us, but also recognize and appreciate even the smallest.

It is my intention to offend or embarrass no one. Therefore, some of the names have been changed to protect the innocent—or the guilty. And, frankly, a few of the names—very few—aren't correct because I couldn't come up with them.

We all have *God in the Rearview Mirror* stories; and I hope this book will jog your memory about your own, and that you will enjoy and benefit from mine.

## Chapter One

# KINDNESS COUNTS

HEY WERE THE neighbors across the street. I didn't know them, but to my young eyes they looked like an ordinary, everyday, middle-aged couple. Did they have any idea of the impact their generosity would have on me? If they did, there was definitely no way for them to know how long lasting that impact would be.

It was nearing Christmas. Because of a farm accident, my dad had been in the hospital hundreds of miles away much of the time for months. Money was tight and Mama and my older sister, Renelda, were working long hours at the local hotel and restaurant to keep food on the table.

Surprisingly, when Christmas morning arrived there were packages. When I tore away the paper from my gift, the rosy face of a doll was staring at me. Though in perfect condition, I was aware she wasn't new and I was, truthfully, a little disappointed. Modern dolls had soft rubbery bodies but hers was cloth. She had a beautiful face; and as I began to play with her, I fell in love. Her eyes would close when I laid her down; and when I tipped her backwards she would say, "Mama." Her pretty white dress and bonnet were handmade by my mother. Included in the package besides the other clothes Mama had made was a little blue jumpsuit. I could tell it wasn't home sewn. Mama told us our gifts had come via the kindness of our neighbors. Though no one said, I wondered who had given Dolly. It wasn't long before I would find out.

My grandparents lived across the street from us, too. For one reason or another, my siblings and I frequented the alley behind their house. Shortly after Christmas while heading up the alley toward my grandparents back yard, I spotted something lying next to their neighbor's trash can. It was a little blue bonnet missing a string. It matched perfectly the jumpsuit that had accompanied my doll. So, now I knew. *They* were the ones. This ordinary, everyday, middle-aged couple had donated Dolly to a family going through tough times. One small act of kindness had brought joy to this pint-sized girl. I will never know if Dolly was of value to them, only that she was special to me.

I still have Dolly. She is wearing her little white dress. The blue jumpsuit and bonnet with one string are folded in a drawer near her. She is *still* special to me.

When that neighbor couple look in their rearview mirror they may or may not remember giving the doll away. But in my rearview mirror that act of kindness has significance and supports the lesson I've learned in life and will, hopefully, never forget. God can use even the smallest kind action for His glory, even if we never become aware of its importance.

> Let your good deeds shine out for all to see, so that everyone will praise your heavenly Father.
> —MATTHEW 5:16, NLT

## Chapter Two

# Son Shine

URGERY WAS OVER, and I was looking forward to getting on with life. The tests on my kidney had not been good, and my fuzzy mind tried to grasp Dr. Matthew's words: "Your kidney was worse than we thought," he told us. "It was too bad to save." With sterile emotion he added the words that hit me like a punch in the stomach. "I caution you that another pregnancy would be a major health risk."

Tears didn't come right then, but an increased thankfulness welled up in me for our eighteen-month-old daughter, Pamela. And taking Dr. Matthews words as gospel, soon my husband Paul and I resigned ourselves to the idea that I wouldn't give birth to another child.

As we went on with life, right before Pamela's third birthday God provided a great job opportunity for Paul in his home state of Colorado. With that move from Nebraska to Colorado came a new and exciting church. Through the Spirit-led Bible teaching, we began to gain a better understanding of God, His love, and His goodness. Along with many other scriptures, Psalm 37:4 came alive to us:

> Delight yourself in the LORD, and he will give you
> the desires of your heart.
>
> —PSALM 37:4, ESV

Something started to stir inside. Though adoption had been a blessing for a number of our friends, the desire to bear another child began to incubate in my soul—not only to fill *my* empty arms, but to have a son for Paul. Because of his love for adventure and the things he enjoyed, I felt sadness at the thought of him going through life without a son. The fear that had been active in us began to subside, and faith started to grow. I decided to ask God for a son and believe that He would bring it to pass. About six months later I became pregnant. Morning sickness was my constant companion for several months and dehydration threatened, but I carried the baby with no major complications. Dr. Hinman, our family doctor, was wonderful as he, Paul, and the Lord watched over me during the pregnancy.

Without ultrasound available to us, the sex of our baby was a mystery. Paul was concerned that I had zeroed in on having a son, and I can't say that I never had a moment of doubt. As our nursery was being prepared, I bought an adorable baby boy outfit and laid it in the bed ready for the trip home from the hospital. Even though I didn't buy the "boy" announcements I'd picked out, in my heart I knew what my prayer had been to God.

A little more than two weeks before my due date shortly after midnight the birth pangs began. We made arrangements for Pamela and headed for the hospital. With Paul by my side during a night of labor, I was finally wheeled into the delivery room. Paul's vantage point was from a window where he could see my face and also the birth. At the moment of delivery, I looked and saw his glowing smile and before Dr. Hinman could utter the words I knew we had our son.

We are grateful for our daughter, Pamela. She has been a tremendous blessing and is one of my best friends. And what about our son? He is now Dr. Kelly Henry with a beautiful wife and the father of our three gorgeous grandchildren. The thought of our lives without them is impossible to imagine.

At one point having another child looked bleak. Physically I was weak, fear possessed us, and our faith was small. But God knew our future. In His grace and mercy, He directed our steps and brought us to a place where we could believe His Word. And as we look in the rearview mirror, we have a small glimpse of what God must have felt when He said:

> This is my Son, whom I love; with him I am well pleased.
>
> —MATTHEW 17:5, NIV

## Chapter Three

# SMARTER THAN YOU THINK

I N THE BARBER chair I sat hearing the beautician down the way. I swear she should have been a blonde. I don't remember her name. Maybe I never knew it, but her incessant silly chatter was nothing new. I'd heard it each time I went for a haircut, and my impression had always been the same—Ms. Dingy! But that day as Sheri worked on cutting my hair, I listened as Ms. D. announced that she had gotten her real estate license. "You've got to be kidding," I grumbled to myself, "*She* got her real estate license?"

Paul's brother, Ken, had been in the real estate business for quite some time, and it interested me greatly. But he was a smart guy, and I had heard about the Colorado real estate test. Everyone I had talked to told me it was very challenging. I hadn't been in school for quite a few years, and I had no confidence that I could pass the difficult test. But that day in the beauty shop my mind was changed.

"If *she* can pass that test and get a license, I can certainly do it," I told myself.

But there were other complications. I had two small children and Paul's work schedule was crazy. Besides that, I discovered shortly that the nearest real estate prep school was in the Denver area, which I felt was too far away for me to manage. At that point I had no idea what was going to happen with my newfound confidence.

A short time later an article in the newspaper excited me. One of the real estate prep schools was bringing their classes to Longmont. None of them had ever done that before. It began to look like God was making a way just for me.

I signed up and took the classes. The contract verbiage was mind-boggling—like learning a foreign language, but I made it through. However, there was still the big state test to pass. The day came and I felt fairly good about how it went. I then waited impatiently for the results which would come weeks later. Before they arrived, I had a dream one night. In the dream a score appeared on the test. It was a passing grade and I was relieved. But was it wishful thinking or actually from the Lord? When the results arrived, it was exactly what was in the dream.

With license in hand, who would I work for? My hours definitely needed to be flexible with needing to care for the children and Paul's unusual work schedule. A Realtor acquaintance from church introduced me to Bob Grigsby, an intelligent, pleasant man twenty years my senior. He agreed to hire me and an excellent ten-year relationship began with Grigsby Realty. It was a perfect fit. God blessed us with a good supplemental income from my newfound profession—a profession that earlier seemed impossible.

The sequence of events God arranged for my career in real estate was nothing short of amazing to me. He first used a divine appointment at a beauty shop. Next He arranged schooling less than two miles from my front door. He helped me pass the difficult test and even told me my grade ahead of time. And then He completed it all by allowing me to work at Grigsby Realty, an ideal place for my situation.

When I lacked confidence to even get started, I never imagined I would look in the rearview mirror years later and see how God's hand worked so wonderfully clear on my behalf.

## Chapter Four

# A Season for Everything

W E'RE GOING TO need you to do our tax return this time," I announced to Bill Kee, a friend and tax professional we had known for at least a decade. Our return had been fairly simple until the last couple of years when the necessity arose to add one thing or another to it.

Asking what the addition was, Bill encouraged, "It's just one more form, LaVila. You can do it." And then, as usual, he began the explanation.

After the same scenario with Bill for the next couple of years, the complication for the new tax season seemed more than I wanted to deal with. This time I decided to bypass Bill's optimistic attitude about my tax return preparation abilities and we took our paperwork to another professional.

My relief was short-lived when we viewed our completed return. From the small amount of research I'd done on our new tax complication, it appeared she had handled it incorrectly. After some discussion and relinquishing my research, our tax return was corrected—but we still received a hefty bill. So much for *that* plan!

"Something is wrong with this picture," I told myself. My mind began to wonder. Was Bill right? Maybe I did have an aptitude for tax work.

Since real estate was rather sluggish, I decided to take a tax class from a national tax organization. At the conclusion of the class, they hired me to prepare returns in one of their local offices for that tax season. I soon learned there was a lot about tax work I enjoyed, but also I learned I didn't like working for that particular employer. With Bill's encouragement, I decided to take things to another level.

Bill was an accountant and what is called an enrolled agent. I had never heard of such a thing and have since found very few others have either. To become an enrolled agent, Bill explained, you had to take a difficult four-part government tax test. All four parts had to be passed in a consecutive two-year period. (Requirements have changed somewhat since then.) As an enrolled agent, you have the right to represent clients before the IRS just as though you are an attorney or a certified public accountant (CPA).

With the real estate license experience behind me, this challenge didn't seem quite as daunting. Having no idea if success would come about, I decided to give it a try anyway.

After pouring over tax guides and a mound of material from Bill, the test day came. Studying hard for the parts that dealt with personal tax returns—which I was more familiar with—a surprise greeted me when the score on one of the business portions was nearly passing. But, "nearly" wasn't enough. So the following year after blood and sweat (but I don't think any tears), the test was behind me and the goal was complete: My enrolled agent license was a reality.

It couldn't have come at a better time. The real estate market in Colorado was in the tank just as my career as a tax professional took off. The house we had built years earlier had an ideal business office right inside the front door. The beautiful little sign that matched our house was hung from hooks on the front porch, and Family Tax Service was born. When one stream of revenue all but dried up, another one had sprung forth.

Once again as I looked in the rearview mirror, God's hand of direction and provision was evident. And along the way it didn't seem strange that for several years Bill hired me to do tax work for him.

# Chapter Five

# DISCORD STRIKES

I'M NOT GOING to be a Christian anymore!" I said it, and I wasn't sorry. Things had been too hard, and it seemed that God was nowhere to be found. Why even try any longer?

The air traffic controllers had gone on strike. As an ATC supervisor, Paul was right in the middle of the turmoil. After President Reagan fired those who didn't go back to work, there were double shifts with no days off for weeks on end, picket lines to cross, and threats of physical violence to both workers and their families. Paul had even found a death threat in his pickup that was supposedly in a secured area. But worst of all were the feelings of betrayal and the longtime friendships lost. The stress on the community was horrendous and our marriage reminded me of that picture you've seen of a frazzled cat with the caption that reads: "I've only got one nerve left—and you're on it!"

And the church that was once our haven had its own set of problems. Controversy with the city over a building permit had made local headlines and the disagreement between the city council and church leadership had gotten ugly. There was very little love, joy, and peace going on in our lives. Strife and division were rampant.

And, sometimes if you're standing on the edge, it takes just a little shove to push you over the cliff. An ongoing unexplainable mechanical problem with our car did the trick. After several trips to the repair shop, for no apparent reason it had quit again—this time in the street in front of our house. We tried to push it up the incline of the driveway into the garage without success; and after our yelling match was over, something inside me broke. In frustration and emotional exhaustion, I took my wounds and headed for the house in disgust.

"I'm not going to be a Christian anymore!" I had uttered the words and I meant it! As I lay there on my bed in the silence waiting and almost hoping for a bolt of lightning to come streaming through the window and strike me dead, something totally unexpected happened.

From deep within a voice spoke. "It's too late," it whispered. "I'm already here."

I was surprised, but I knew *who* it was: the Holy Spirit. According to God's Word, He had come to live in me when I was born again. I'd heard Him before, but it had been a while. Unfortunately, I had allowed my present stress-saturated situation to drown out the One who wanted to do the most for me. But He had spoken—and I heard. He wasn't angry. His voice was sweet. Right then God's light and love penetrated the darkness in my heart, and I knew He was with us and bigger than the troubles that had overwhelmed us. From that point slowly I began to rise out of the ashes. Scriptures started to come alive again as I looked to them for help:

> Many are the afflictions of the righteous: but the LORD delivereth him out of them all.
>
> —PSALMS 34:19

> What shall we then say to these things? If God be
> for us, who can be against us?
>
> —ROMANS 8:31

Shortly our friends Bill and Carole insisted, and kept insisting, we try their new church. Absolutely not in the mood and frankly just to silence them, we went. Our very first Sunday the presence of God was thick in the atmosphere and we felt like dry brittle sponges soaking in warm soothing water. As we continued to attend, our injured and decimated souls were once again receiving the refreshing salve of the Word and the Spirit on a regular basis. And that church—Resurrection Fellowship—was our home for the next twenty-one years.

It wasn't until we found help that we realized how far from God we had strayed and how wounded we had become. The sermon subject escapes me, but I remember the Sunday when I felt fully recovered from the spiritual damage I had allowed. It was a wonderful day.

And what happened with the rest of the situation?

Most of the air traffic controllers President Reagan fired never returned to work. Though it took quite some time, eventually chaos returned to calmness and a new group of trained air traffic controllers took their places.

Sadly, our former church took quite a few years to fully recover. And though that disappointed us, we were grateful for the annoying persistence of our friends Bill and Carole. As we look in the rearview mirror, we see the hand of the Lord in their actions, directing us to a new church—a church that happened to be our place of healing.

## Chapter Six

# SECOND CHANCES

THE DELIVERY TRUCK had arrived with the stove and refrigerator for our newly remodeled kitchen. Though grateful, I couldn't seem to get over my nagging disappointment. The kitchen had never been my favorite room in the house. There was even a joke we'd heard years ago that made light of my lack of more-than-basic culinary skills. Paul would declare with a smile, "She told me when we got married that she would be good in one room of the house and I could choose." And though that always got a laugh, I was hoping the new kitchen would spur me on to a greater desire to cultivate my cooking skills.

The shopping trip for the new appliances had come a few days earlier. Our purchases included my first side-by-side refrigerator in beautiful gleaming white with black trim. The delivery men set it in place and I opened the doors to examine the interior and began to organize its contents in my mind.

Shortly, my thoughts drifted to the next appliance they would be unloading. Regret was repressing the enthusiasm that I should have been enjoying. After cleaning burners for so many years, this time I had badly wanted a smooth-top range. My frugal nature had succumbed to the electric range that had been on the best sale—one with burners. If I had changed my mind at that point, it would have meant a large additional delivery charge; and the new kitchen had already stretched our budget as far as we wanted to go. "I made the decision and I'll live with it," I told myself. There were certainly more important things in life.

One of the delivery men reappeared in the kitchen. "We aren't going to be able to install your range," he announced. "The one on the truck has a big dent in the side."

Instantly my thoughts connected with the Lord. Thankfully, I didn't hear Him declare in a booming voice or even in a still-small voice, "That's what you get, lady, for your ungrateful attitude. There will be no new stove for you today." Instead, it was almost as though I could see His kind face and hear Him saying, "I know how much you wanted the smooth-top stove, Child, and I'm making a way for that to happen."

And it did. The delivery truck had barely driven out of sight when I hurried to the store to make a new choice a smooth-top range.

Some may say the delivered appliance had a dent because sometimes those things just happen, and I suppose they do. But I perceived it differently. It can be little things that allow us to understand how much God cares about every aspect of our lives. Looking at the big picture it was a seemingly small and insignificant incident, but it felt huge to me that day. The God who created the universe cared about the details of this young homemaker's existence. He cared enough to make a way to recover from a regrettable decision and bring her the desires of her heart, even in the room of the house where she was not particularly proficient. That day I saw Him in the rearview mirror.

## Chapter Seven

# IN-LAWS OR OUTLAWS

ID YOU HEAR about the two cannibals talking? One said to the other, "I hate my mother-in-law." "Then just eat the noodles," was the reply. (You'll get it later.)

As I stood in the living area of my mother-in-law's home, I could hear her talking on the phone. It was one of my husband's old girlfriends—someone known to his family for most of her life. Part of Ruby's end of the conversation went something like this: "I believe he married her on the rebound because she looks like you." And later they even discussed my dress size!

In the words of Mr. T., "I'm sorry, but I ain't Jesus." And though I didn't make a big scene at the time, I was sizzling on the inside. *How dare she talk to Paul's ex-girlfriend about me like that, and with me standing in the same room! Did she think I was deaf or what?*

Thus started the turbulent beginning of my relationship with Ruby B. Henry.

We saw each other very few times the first years Paul and I were married, and that was fine with me. But when we moved from Nebraska and Paul took the air traffic control position in Longmont, Colorado, things changed. Though I wasn't always excited about it, quite often on Paul's days off we would pack up and make the trek to Fruita on the other side of the mountains to visit his family.

It was then Ruby and I began to know each other, and my opinion of her started to soften. She was the hardest working women I had ever met; and when most of us were enjoying the conveniences we took for granted, Paul's parents' house was still being heated by wood. Up early, Ruby would start a fire in the cook-stove and the fireplace to warm the house and begin breakfast. And just to mention a few other things, there was the care for the foster children they had taken in, sewing clothing, and canning and freezing all kinds of vegetables she had grown in her huge garden. Those things were only a start.

But it wasn't her work you needed to watch out for, it was her tongue. Honest to a fault, whatever she said you knew she believed it to be true. But there was no apparent filter. In those early years, thinking it and saying it seemed to be one and the same to her.

She wasn't a complainer, and it took quite some time to learn she was one of fourteen siblings and had come from a turbulent and abusive home. At the age of nine-teen with gangrene throughout her abdomen, she had been sent home from the hospital to die when the Lord miraculously healed her. (That's a wonderful story of its own.) Shortly she became a minister of the gospel criss-crossing the United States as an evangelist giving her testimony of God's healing power.

It was during one of those meetings she met Paul's dad, Harold. His wife Pauline had died of polio the year before, leaving him with two small boys, ages three and four. After a short courtship, they were married and a year later Paul's sister Linda was born. Though

Ruby continued to minister locally, because of her new responsibilities, her life as an evangelist was greatly diminished. But her love for the Lord and the Word of God wasn't. It became a bond between us because I love God's Word, too. And though it wasn't overnight, somewhere along the way we became friends. I grew to appreciate her honesty. It was refreshing to know I never had to wonder if she was telling the truth. Though it usually wasn't sugarcoated, it was *always* the truth as she understood it.

I began to look forward to our trips to visit. After everyone else was in bed, many times we would stay up until the wee hours of the morning counseling each other when problems arose in our lives and discussing new things we had learned from the Bible. She allowed me to speak to her with the same unvarnished truth she spoke to me—and it worked for us both.

A couple of years before her trip to heaven, my grieving began. Her thoughts were no longer clear and Bible stories were mixed together. Sharing our learning experiences or our problems and solutions was no longer an option. And though our intimate times were gone—and I missed them terribly—my dearly loved friend was still here. And even though her mind was failing her, I could tell she still felt the bond between us. When she exited this life to her heavenly reward, it was a comfort to know I would see my precious mother-in-law again—once more totally intact. And I was grateful.

It is hard to fathom how such a rough start could be turned into a rich blessing. It was definitely by the grace of God. There is a lesson in it that can be applied to many other areas of our lives. It is this: how something begins *never* dictates the ending. When we keep God in the equation, anything is possible. And through my forty-four-year relationship with Ruby B. Henry, that truth is very clear to me in my rearview mirror.

## Chapter Eight

# FREE AT LAST

THIS CANNOT BE true," I emphatically told myself after reading the newspaper article. "Surely I would have already heard this from someone if it were accurate." It was all about reducing your mortgage debt and sounded *far* too simple to be real and too good to be true.

I needed to check it out.

It required an amortization schedule, and I was pretty sure we hadn't received one for our thirty-year home loan. Upon request our mortgage company supplied it; and much to my surprise, the article was correct. The higher the interest rate, the more dramatic the results; but by simply paying, in addition to the regular payment, the amount going to principal for the next month, over the life of the loan a mortgage can be cut in half. The financial benefits outweigh the cost tremendously. Of course banks know this; but in that "truth vs ignorance" moment, it became very clear: Banks don't reveal their secrets. They are there to make money—from all of *us*.

Paul and I had already been getting some teaching about finances from our church. But, we were the typical American family. Included in our debt was our home, cars, credit cards—and occasionally a personal loan from the bank for something, no doubt, we felt we couldn't live without.

Do you know what "floating a check" means? With the electronics these days I assume it would be harder to do, but for years our money would usually be gone three or four days before the next payday. Almost every time we would write a check on Friday knowing that it wouldn't get to the bank until Monday when the new paycheck would be there. (We floated a check.) Eventually this thought came to us: *If we are always consistently the same amount behind every week, why can't we be consistently ahead that much?* We had formed a bad habit, and we decided to break it. Soon we found we were able to have a balance left in the bank before payday. Things were coming together.

And, after reading that newspaper article, something else was simmering in my mind. Could we become debt free? I started to pray about it, and soon Paul was on board, too. We had been faithful givers almost since day one of our marriage; and when we were ready to listen, it felt like God was using that commitment to take us to a higher level in our finances. We were certainly acquainted with the scripture in Malachi:

> Bring the full tithe into the storehouse, that there may be food in my house. And thereby put me to the test, says the LORD of hosts, if I will not open the windows of heaven for you and pour down for you a blessing until there is no more need.
>
> —MALACHI 3:10, ESV

We also knew we weren't there yet. Our needs were being met, but our hearts told us there could be more.

Over a period of time, we gained additional financial wisdom and knowledge and put it into action. Slowly but surely our debt was reduced. At times God even provided beyond our paychecks. And finally it was done. We were debt free!

Was it easy? Not always. Was it worth it? Absolutely! What a wonderful feeling! Our resources no longer went toward paying interest on loans. It produced a freedom those laden with debt will probably never know. It has caused us to be able to go places and experience things that seemed out of reach. And seeing what God has done for us makes giving more of a joy than ever.

As we look in the rearview mirror, along with His faithful supply, God taught us to use our resources with greater wisdom and discretion.

And there is good news! We are not special people. God will do the same for anyone.

## Chapter Nine

# LET THE SHOW BEGIN

N**O, YOU WILL** not be allowed to broadcast the services of Resurrection Fellowship on our local cable TV station here in Longmont," we were told. "They" had tried and failed. I'm not sure who "they" from the church were, but that was how it was conveyed to us.

This situation was certainly of interest, because we lived in Longmont but attended Resurrection Fellowship in the neighboring town of Loveland, and we weren't alone. At that time we knew there were at least four hundred other people who drove the twenty-some miles to attend services at Resurrection Fellowship, fondly known as Rez.

Rez was flourishing like a plant on Miracle Gro, and we hated missing even one service. It would be great to have it aired in town—not only for those of us who attended Rez, but also to expose the rest of our community to the teaching that was feeding our souls and spirits so wonderfully.

A trip to Longmont's Channel 3, our local public access channel, seemed in order. During my visit I received the same answer about airing Rez's program. No! Though nothing had changed there, I gained some information. The TV studio shared its quarters with the Career Development Center and CDC would soon be offering beginning TV classes to the general public. Signing up seemed the thing to do.

It was a small class; and though I wasn't "old" at the time, I was one of the oldest in the group. Nearly all of my classmates were young people hoping to somehow break in to the TV profession. Along with our instruction we were each required to write our own mini TV segment and, with the help of our classmates, film and edit it. Mr. Boyington, a sturdy, jolly man was our instructor. He was patient and seemed truly entertained by our amateur scripts and attempts at humor. Over the weeks our writing, camera, and lighting instruction progressed to the editing room. Editing was painstakingly slow as we poured over our tapes and attempted to cut on the exact frame we intended in order to come up with our wonderful little mini programs without glitches. (Well, at least *we* thought they were wonderful.) The editing turned out to be an amazing experience. I loved it. Lost in time, what took hours always seemed like minutes.

Over the weeks I got to know the young Channel 3 TV crew. There was Jim W., the cheery-faced news anchor who also announced high school sports. Jim P. and Amy were his competent coworkers. Before all was said and done, there turned out to be a bonus for me. Since I was a tax professional, I was asked to make some five minute "tax tip" segments to air in between programs. It was great fun.

The classes were over sooner than I wanted, but I hadn't forgotten the mission. Why wouldn't they let Rez air the church program? There seemed to be no concrete reason. The TV crew I'd gotten to know added their voices to mine, and the "powers that be" agreed to air Rez's church service tape each week. Their only requirement was that we be responsible to deliver it and have it there ahead of time.

The program turned out to be a blessing to many. Not only for those of us who occasionally had to miss services, but over the years we heard frequent reports of its impact on the lives of others who watched.

As I looked in the rearview mirror, I saw how God took someone with absolutely no prior skill to accomplish what He wanted done. And He will even let that person have fun doing it. How can I be sure of that? I have firsthand experience.

## Chapter Ten

# MEETING AT THE TOP

IT WAS WELL past the time when they should have returned. I sat in the lobby of the famous hot springs pool in Glenwood Springs, Colorado, waiting for Paul and our nephew Shane. Not usually accompanying Paul on those adventures, I had gone with him and agreed to stay in Glenwood while he and Shane conquered another mountain.

Paul was on a quest to climb all fifty-four of the 14,000 foot mountains in Colorado. Though our son, Kelly, had been his climbing companion on many, Shane was with him that day.

After they left, sleeping in felt good, and I later had time to wander the streets and visit some of the quaint shops that line the picturesque avenues of Glenwood Springs. Through his research and experience, Paul knew approximately what time he and Shane would return. Our agreement was to meet at the hot springs pool, and I was there.

The time of his expected arrival was long past, and worry threatened. Thoughts began to pour through my head: *Had one of them fallen? If something had happened and they didn't return, who should I contact? How much longer should I wait?*

Paul's desire to accomplish this goal hadn't set well with me. Why would anyone want to put themselves in those dangerous situations on purpose? It didn't make sense, but it seemed he was made for this quest—often climbing with the ease of a mountain goat. Besides, we always prayed over the trips and he had promised he would take no unnecessary risks. He'd already proved that a couple of times by cancelling after arriving at the base of a mountain and finding weather conditions weren't conducive for a safe climb.

That was all well and good, but there I was in a town where I knew no one—waiting and waiting and waiting some more.

I prayed,

> *Lord, please keep them safe, and give me Your peace. I know Your Word says not to worry or fret, so I'm making a conscious effort not to be caught up in it. Direct me in whatever I need to know or do.*

"Will LaVila Henry please come to the ticket booth?" the loudspeaker blared, "You have a phone call." They pronounced my name incorrectly, but I was accustomed to that and knew the summons was for me. Paul was the only one who was aware of my location. This had to be either from him or about him.

Taking the phone and greeting the caller, I heard, "Mrs. Henry, this is the sheriff's office."

❀ ❀ ❀

For Paul, this climb hadn't required the predawn start like so many before it. However, Shane had left before dawn and driven over an hour from his home to meet

Paul in Glenwood Springs. After another hour of winding mountain roads, 14,279-foot Castle Peak—the ninth highest summit in the Rocky Mountains—was looming in front of them.

It was Paul's twenty-ninth fourteener. He had climbed several of them more than once usually taking novices on their first mountain expeditions. I'd even given Grays Peak a try. After my heart rate hit around two hundred beats a minute two-thirds of the way to the summit, I gave it up and headed back to the trail head. Mountain climbing wasn't for me.

But Paul thrived on it. By the time he was looking up at Castle Peak, his trusty climbing boots were well broken in—with just the right amount of comfort but still plenty of traction. His well-worn backpack had sufficient water and food for the climb, as well as proper clothing and emergency supplies. There needed to be a balance between the weight he carried and safety. He had it down to a science.

The weather was good, and it looked like it would be a rather routine trip. However, he never tired of the beauty and the exhilaration he felt when he reached the summit, always taking at least a few minutes to capture the spectacular view. That was never routine.

Following the difficult and increasingly steep trail, they stopped at about 13,400 feet to rest and rehydrate. As they stood there, Paul caught a glimpse of two other climbers—the only ones they had seen on the mountain that day. The couple were on a narrow, jagged ridgeline about 350 feet above them. "I'd never climb that ridgeline," Paul commented to Shane, "It's too risky."

As they observed the climbers negotiate the difficult terrain, the unthinkable happened. One of the two climbers lost footing and began to fall. In horror Paul and Shane watched as she dropped several stories, bounced off the rock face a couple times and came to rest on a ledge not far off the route they were following. Paul and Shane were much closer than her partner and they quickly made their way up to the ledge.

Screaming in pain with her helmet still intact and daypack on her back, her left leg was grotesquely twisted under her. Another obvious wound was a gash on her forehead and they could tell there were other severe injuries. Happy she hadn't been killed in the fall, with the first aid supplies they had with them, they made her as comfortable as possible without moving her. Wearing shorts and having no coat, the shaded ledge made the cool high altitude seem even colder, and Paul covered her with his jacket and spare climbing pants.

After making his way off the jagged ridge and down the steep slope, her partner finally arrived. It was in the early days of cell phones, and he had one. However, there was no signal. Taking the phone, Paul trekked down the trail to a clearing two thousand feet below. There he found reception and called for help. But help wasn't close. He was told it would be more than two hours before search and rescue could arrive. He returned to the ledge with the news.

Making conversation to pass the time and keep her awake and alert, among other things Paul learned her name was Jamie. In what seemed like an eternity, a little less than five hours after the fall they could see two men making their way up the incline. Search and rescue had arrived. They had soon stabilized her neck and her leg and secured her to the rescue board they had brought with them. Because of the difficult terrain and the severity of Jamie's injuries, Paul and Shane joined them as they slid and then carried her as gently as possible down the steep rocky trail to the waiting ambulance.

❋ ❋ ❋

Back at the pool I was taking the call.

"Mrs. Henry, this is the sheriff's office," he reported. "Your husband asked me to call and tell you he is okay."

Relief flooded my soul.

"Do you know when I can expect him back?" I questioned.

"He should be back in an hour or so," he replied.

❋ ❋ ❋

As I look in the rearview mirror, I see that for a few hours I—once again—had the opportunity to cast my care on the Lord, trust Him with my circumstances, and not let worry overwhelm me.

And what about Jamie? That day on a remote mountain, God had two men in exactly the right place at exactly the right time to help save her life. Later we learned she fully recovered, and about a year after the fall a package from Jamie arrived in the mail. It was Paul's climbing jacket and extra pants.

My times are in your hands.

—PSALMS 31:15, NIV

## Chapter Eleven

# CAUTION TO THE WIND

W E WERE WELL on our way; but as we reached the outskirts of Colorado Springs, we heard and felt the left rear tire explode. *Could anything else go wrong?* I thought.

"We're not going to make the flight in time," Bob agonized. "I'm going to have to call my cousin and he will need to send another car just so we can make it back to Denver."

My immediate thought was: *This guy flies a multimillion dollar airplane and he doesn't know how to change a tire?*

It had been an unusual experience from the beginning. I was headed out to spend a few days with our daughter, Pamela, in Houston. For the first and only time ever, Paul had driven me the hour to Denver International Airport (DIA) and left me there by myself. Pamela's airline job had afforded us great benefits, but our status was always the same—stand-by. Until then, if I was going by myself Paul would hang around to make sure I had gotten on the airplane. However, his work schedule didn't allow him to stay that evening.

The weather wasn't great, but neither of us thought it was bad enough to cause any kind of problem—certainly not bad enough to cancel flights. However, the weather began to deteriorate steadily. There were several others in my same situation. As they announced delay after delay and the moments ticked on, some of us who were on stand-by spoke a few words in passing. Among others there was Bob, a pilot doing his best to be on time for his next flight assignment, along with his wife, Karla, and their newborn baby.

Finally, the news came that the flight had been cancelled. Not only our flight, but the weather had gotten bad enough that there would be no more flights that night. As I sat there wondering what I was going to do, Bob approached. "The flights out of Colorado Springs are still running," he informed me. "My cousin manages a rental car company. He said we could get a car for free to go to Colorado Springs. Do you want to go with us?" Ashley, a flight attendant with the same urgency to get to work had already accepted the offer.

In that crazy moment and without much hesitation I answered, "Yes." Somehow right then it seemed the correct thing to do and we headed out into the weather. I managed to call Paul from the car rental company and tell him my decision. (Cell phones were a thing of the future.)

As we headed south on I-25 out of Denver, the realization hit me that Karla was stressed to the limit and was having a difficult time taking care of her baby. Ashley and I took over.

The interstate wasn't too bad, and it looked like we could get to the airport for the last flight to Houston with a little time to spare. But, as we reached the north end of Colorado Springs, the evening's nightmare seemed to be continuing. There we sat with a flat tire.

The next words out of my mouth surprised even me. "Hey, I'm not an old farm girl for nothing. Let's get out and change the tire."

Before I knew it Bob and I were beside the interstate with cars whipping our clothing as they zipped by a few feet away. And the old farm girl was telling the young city pilot what to do. Thankfully it went off without a hitch. As we limped along on the non-full-size spare tire, we proceeded to the Colorado Springs airport in time to board the flight. We had made it. We were on the last commercial airplane leaving from Colorado to Houston that night.

It was a bizarre occasion with decisions I had never made before or since. I was grateful to get to Houston to visit Pamela. But the Word of God says this:

> Share each other's burdens, and in this way obey
> the law of Christ.
> —GALATIANS 6:2, NLT

I didn't start out knowing Bob, Karla, or Ashley's burdens that night, but God did. And though I hadn't met them before and haven't seen them since, as I look in the rearview mirror, could it be that God placed a person strategically to comfort and care for the baby of a stressed-out mom and also help a young pilot and flight attendant get to work on time? Maybe so.

# ⁓ Chapter Twelve ⁓

# 911

I HAVE A MESSAGE from your daughter," the lady on the phone stated. "She wants me to tell you she is fine and she is in Gander, Newfoundland."

My eyes filled with tears as I spoke. "Is there a number where I can reach her?"

"Let me see if I can patch you through." It was my first indication I was speaking to an operator. After a couple of minutes, the phone line went dead and then rang again. It was the same lady. "Let me try once more," she insisted. After the third attempt I heard Pamela's voice come on the line. Through our sobs we began to convey our messages to each other.

It was September 11, 2001.

That morning as I emerged from upstairs, Paul reported, "A plane just flew into one of the twin towers in New York."

As I stood there in the middle of the family room the unthinkable happened and we both watched in disbelief as another plane exploded into the side of the second tower. From then on, like everyone else, we were riveted to the TV waiting to hear the latest news.

"Where's Pamela," Paul asked.

"She's coming home from London today, but I don't know which flight she's on." As of yet, no one knew how widespread the hijacking was, and we were definitely concerned.

Shortly one of Pamela's coworkers called. She said she would check the schedule and find out Pamela's flight number and call us back—and she did. With that information in hand, Paul contacted his former colleagues at the air traffic control center and asked if they would locate the airplane. From all indications it was flying its normal route from London. However, soon the government ordered all airplanes out of the sky and we had no idea where Pamela would end up.

Although at that point we had no reason to believe anything other than she was safe, I longed to hear her voice; and with the help of the kindhearted and persistent Canadian telephone operator, my prayer had been answered. Pamela explained that she was still on the airplane, and wanting to be strong for the passengers, tried not to cry—though neither of us passed that test very well. Theirs was one of more than thirty-five jetliners carrying over six thousand passengers that had landed at the airport in Gander nearly doubling the town's population. Because of the circumstances, safety measures were extreme and all passengers and crews were ordered to stay onboard until the necessary security was intact. News for those on the airplane was sketchy, and we did our best to fill her in quickly on what we had heard. Our conversation was short but comforting to us all.

I was awakened at 2:00 a.m. The phone was ringing. Immediately I thought it was Pamela—and I was right. She and the rest of the crew and the passengers were still on the plane. Most were sleeping. Earlier, a few had gotten a connection through the airplane phones. Since Pamela had nothing else to do, she dialed our number over and over again. Finally it rang. This time we had a chance for a longer conversation. Several aspects of her flight had been good—if there was such a thing in that 24-hour period. Her flight hadn't been full, so most people were able to find somewhere to rest. Unlike many of the flights ending up at Gander, because of their light load, they had an adequate amount of water and toilets hadn't overflowed. News still being minimal, I filled her in on what we had learned during the day.

After being on the airplane for more than thirty hours, it was finally their turn to disembark and go through customs. Pamela was suffering from a fever and was whisked away from her crew to medical personnel. Feeling alone and not knowing if she would be reunited with her colleagues, the kindness of her new hosts soon became apparent. Before long she had been checked, given a prescription without cost, and driven to the hotel where her crew was staying.

I don't know who besides the Lord was in charge of organizing what happened in Gander that week, but the people of the area followed the lead in a remarkable way. Though the school bus drivers had been on strike, they suspended their disagreement. The passengers were carried to local schools, fire stations, and auditoriums in Gander and neighboring towns where makeshift beds were made available and meals were delivered, keeping their surprise guests fed. People opened their own homes to the elderly, infirm, and mothers traveling alone with their infants. Per a request to the Red Cross, during their stay Pamela and her crew were taken to visit and encourage their passengers. Finally, on September 15th they were allowed to board their airplane and continue their flight to its original destination in Houston.

On September 11, 2001, we didn't have to wonder if there was an evil enemy at work in this world or that there were those who would obey his commands. However, there were others who showed us by their deeds the lesson of The Good Samaritan to near perfection. The citizens of Gander and the surrounding area were some of those people.

Those of you who are old enough to remember know our nation was changed that day and has never been the same. We experienced to a larger degree—more than ever before—the wrath of young men who had been so terribly deceived as to think they were doing their god a favor by taking the lives of thousands of innocent people.

And though *our* family's inconvenience, fear, and anxiety was *nothing* compared to the life-altering loss of thousands of others, we can see in the rearview mirror how God has brought us and many more past that tragedy. And though far too much evil and deception continues to abound, *our* God's grace much more abounds. And there is still an abundance of those who believe this freedom-giving order from Christ:

> Do to others as you would like them to do to you.
> —LUKE 6:31, NLT

And, thankfully, there is still a multitude of those who live their lives in that way.

## Chapter Thirteen

# SLEEPING BEAUTY

L AVILA, THIS IS Wanda." She sounded strange. It was Sunday morning and we were ready to walk out the door for our drive to church when we got the call.

"Wanda, what's the matter?" I questioned.

"Jim had a heart attack and we're at the hospital." We lived just blocks away and were there within minutes.

Wanda and Jim were longtime friends. We had started attending church together in Longmont nearly the same weekend thirty-three years earlier. At that time they were brand-new believers and we had just moved there for Paul to begin his career in air traffic control. They had no children and neither of us had family in town, so we adopted each other. They were, and still are, Uncle Jim and Aunt Wanda to our kids. However, the years, job changes, and church situations had taken us on different paths and we hadn't seen each other nearly as often as years earlier.

When we got to the hospital, we found Wanda in the waiting room. She looked stunned. Something had gone terribly wrong with the procedure they had done on Jim, and he was in intensive care.

We quickly realized none of their family had been contacted and Wanda had no numbers with her. Though her mind was fuzzy, upon questioning she responded, "I think I can remember my sister-in-law's number." I dialed it. At the worst it would be wrong, but it wasn't. She could contact the rest of the family.

Finally we were allowed to see Jim. He wasn't conscious. There had been a rare reaction to a commonly used medication for heart patients, and after his surgery the doctors were unable to wake him.

When Wanda reiterated the details to us, we knew the Lord had already been at work in the whole situation. Jim's job was unique. He was—and still is at this writing—an expert consultant for putting huge gas tanks into the ground, or taking them out—like those buried at gas stations, airports, etc. He was on the road most of the time driving from job to job across the state. However, the day of the heart attack he was at home. It happened as he was working right in their own front yard. They lived close to the hospital in the opposite direction from us and were able to get there quickly. But as much of a miracle as that seemed, what was supposed to be a simple procedure had turned into a nightmare.

Hours turned into days and days to weeks. During our visits when we spoke to Jim, he would respond restlessly but he could not wake up. The doctors eventually gave Wanda very little hope that he would live, but we prayed and then we prayed again and continued to pray.

After several weeks, Wanda wanted to go to the funeral home. In years past from the early days of our strict faith teaching we would have probably freaked out. We would have told her, "No, we can't do that. It would prove we don't have enough faith for Jim to get well." But actually what it really would have proved is that we had more faith in our faith than faith in our God.

At that point I knew my Father better than that. I just couldn't see Him saying, "That's it! Now you've done it. You've gone to the funeral home and that proves you have no faith, and for sure I will not heal Jim." By then I knew God is good, is always for us and never against us, and He is the God who takes pleasure in the prosperity of His children. Besides, Jim would still have a say in things.

The funeral home visit seemed to ease Wanda's mind, and we all continued to pray and speak God's Word to each other and to Jim. We remembered Abraham and how he "call[ed] those things which be not as though they were" (Rom. 4:17). And we did the same.

As more and more time passed Jim continued to live and his doctors continued researching for solutions. And, of course, we also prayed for the doctors. Finally, they came up with a different medication that was normally used for an unrelated illness and gave it a try—and it *worked.* Jim came to and began to talk. But the ordeal wasn't over. He was still very sick. The hospital was on the route of our three-mile walk, and daily we would stop to visit and check his improvement. After sixty-seven days Jim was released from the hospital, his heart and mind intact.

He and Wanda's faith was stronger than ever. He made some lifestyle changes and began an exercise program and became healthier than he had been in a long time. Many years have passed since that fateful day, and at this writing Jim is still working and doing well. Wanda is grateful God spared her the heartbreak of losing her mate, and we are grateful we still have our friend.

And as we look in the rearview mirror, we see how God carried these dear ones through the valley of the shadow of death and left them better on the other side.

## Chapter Fourteen

# WHO'S YOUR MAMA?

THE WEDDING HAD been beautiful; and my niece, Katie, and her new husband, Tom, seemed truly made for each other. After a drive from the church to the reception, soon the festivities were in full swing. It had been a long time since I had lived in Nebraska, and it was great to see extended family and old friends.

As we gorged on beautiful handmade delicacies and drank punch, I was approached by Roberta, someone I had known when she was a child. She had since grown up, married Mark, one of our former pastor's sons, and had adult children of her own.

"This is my spiritual mother," she stated to her daughter who was with her. My mind immediately whirled to memories from days long gone.

Back then the drive from Bloomfield to Crofton, Nebraska, didn't seem that bad, and my mom sometimes kept me company. I had somehow become acquainted with Child Evangelism Fellowship (CEF), a ministry for children. Though I lived in Bloomfield, my work schedule allowed me to start a CEF meeting each Tuesday after school in the neighboring town of Crofton. We met in a home close to the school and sometimes gathered at picnic tables under the big shade trees in the park. It was great fun with singing, Bible stories, and other activities.

At the age of nineteen I was barely more than a kid myself, but I'd already had practice at this sort of thing. From the time I was a freshman in high school through the months after my senior year, much of the summers of those four years had been spent in the Sandhills of Nebraska teaching vacation Bible school (VBS) in one-room country school houses and churches.

Al and Lucille Perrin were missionaries for the American Sunday School Union serving in the little town of Long Pine where I had lived as a kid and where my grandparents still resided. On the weekends I would stay with Meme and Bapa, and then on Sunday after-noon needed supplies would be packed up and Mr. Perrin would whisk two of us off to a remote location deep in the Sandhills, usually to stay with a local ranch family. We would hold classes for the children of the area Monday through Friday from nine to four. Among other things, we would sing songs and learn stories from the Bible, often using flannel boards. (Are you old enough to remember those? There would be a flannel background typically draped over an easel. You could purchase or make your own pictures of people and other necessary items that had a fuzzy back and would stick to the flannel.) With them we would tell a story from the Bible. Friday evening we'd have an ending program with all the parents invited to be in attendance.

As a rule two teen girls were dropped off at each loca-tion, though I also loved it when Mrs. Connell was my teaching partner. She seemed older to me; but now that I'm not so young, maybe she wasn't that old after all. Whoever I was with, we had a great time; and amaz-ingly, I can't remember ever having any discipline prob-lems with a child during the four years I participated.

Although I'm sure the quality of my teaching lacked much, it was a splendid opportunity and a wonderful experience.

At the age of nineteen, after teaching four years in the Sandhills, starting a CEF meeting seemed an easy thing to do. Using their materials created a sound foundation and generally ten to twenty of us had a joyful time learning about the Lord.

And now, all these decades later I was hearing the words, "This is my spiritual mother." It startled me for a second. Back then teaching those classes didn't seem like a big deal. But here was evidence to the contrary.

Roberta continued, "I was born again during our after-school meetings. That makes you my spiritual mother."

"I'm happy to be your spiritual mother," I affirmed.

Turning to her daughter she announced, "And that makes her your spiritual grandmother." The thought made me smile.

"And I'm happy to have you as my spiritual grand-daughter," was my reply. "I'll take all the spiritual grand-children I can get."

Since then Roberta and I have become friends on Facebook. When I was thinking about this story, I asked for her recollection of that time in her childhood. Here is what she wrote:

> When I was about 8 or 9 some friends invited my sisters and my brother and myself to a Good News Club. It met every week after school for an hour or so. I don't remember the story you told that day, but I do remember that it must have been about birth-days and my birthday was coming up soon. I listened carefully and remember that you explained

that we could have another birthday—that was even more important than our first birthday. I remember being aware that it was so important that I had better choose a second birthday that very day! So when you invited anyone who wanted to pray with you and invite Jesus into their life, I joined you in the hall. That day I became a new creature! I had no idea where that would lead, but I was excited to have the assurance that I was on my way to heaven! You truly are my spiritual "mom." Thank you!

Our conversation at the wedding was a unique moment for me—receiving a glimpse of the fruits of my labor and the faithfulness of God from more than forty years earlier. It was something time had crowded deep into the back of my mind. It proved once again the scripture found in Isaiah 55:11:

> So shall my word be that goeth forth out of my mouth: it shall not return unto me void, but it shall accomplish that which I please, and it shall prosper in the thing whereto I sent it.

God's Word has staying power. He sent His Word to a little girl all those years ago, and it *stayed* in her heart and life. I'm grateful that God was so gracious in allowing me to look in the rearview mirror and see it all fresh and new.

## Chapter Fifteen

# THE HOMETOWN CROWD

**M**Y KNEES WERE shaking a little as I stood on the stage of the building called The Palace— though it didn't really look like one—in the little town of Long Pine, Nebraska, where we lived when I was a kid. It had been a fun celebration. The occasion was my parents' fiftieth wedding anniversary. And though we'd had quite a time getting the old sound system to cooperate, it finally did. Our family had created a slide show and performed music and skits, most with some nostalgic value. As a finale my parents renewed their vows in front of the nearly one hundred and fifty family and friends who had come to help them celebrate.

But now I was doing something God had put on my heart, and thankfully Paul and my siblings were happy to cheer me on. I was glad, because this particular audience made me nervous. It was Jesus Himself who said in Mark 6:4:

> A prophet is not without honour, but in his own country, and among his own kin, and in his own house.

However, I felt it was pretty much a mandate from the Lord. I was supposed to give a salvation message. It was nearly a perfect setting because I was standing on the stage just a few blocks from where I had given my heart to the Lord thirty-some years earlier.

Long Pine had been a hub of activity in its glory days when the railroad had a roundhouse there and a beautiful, stately, white hotel housed hundreds of passengers on a weekly basis; but those days were over. It was already becoming a sleepy little village during my younger years. There were still a few struggling churches with peeling paint on their once beautiful exteriors.

But then several new couples came to town. It was John and Carol Rempel and their colleagues. The word got around they were going to have vacation Bible school (VBS) and a bunch of us showed up. Along with the fun Bible stories and other activities, that week in VBS I heard something new. They asked if any of us wanted to invite Jesus into our hearts, and make Him our Savior. I said yes.

It was the first time I ever remember hearing John 3:16:

> For God so loved the world, that he gave his only begotten Son, that whosoever believeth in him should not perish, but have everlasting life.

Now all those years later, nervously standing on the stage, I told them of my decision a few blocks away and how it had changed and enriched my life. And at the end, those in the audience were invited to join in a prayer asking Jesus to be their Savior, too.

And though to this day the results of that event aren't perfectly clear in the rearview mirror, as I thought of writing about it there is one thing I hadn't considered until I experienced Roberta coming up to me and saying, "This is my spiritual mother." Our family hadn't seen them in decades, but in the audience that day, getting a glimpse of the fruit of their labor from over thirty years earlier were my spiritual parents, John and Carol Rempel.

## Chapter Sixteen

# A LEMON BECOMES LEMONADE

THEY HAD FINALLY installed the stairs to the basement and we had our first chance to check it out. What did we find? Incased in the cement floor a foot away and directly in front of the bottom step was the rough-in plumbing for the bathroom. No, that wasn't where it belonged!

Though we were very excited about building a new house, for nearly a year the city had delayed most of the building permits for this new and popular housing development. We felt we had the go-ahead from the Lord, but nothing seemed to fall easily into place from the day they broke ground. There was the replacing of part of the roof and framing the bathroom window that had been forgotten. Contractual changes to the original plan had not been implemented causing tearing down and rebuilding parts of the house. Those were just a few of the numerous bungles that had taken place.

We found it necessary to keep a watchful eye on construction almost daily. Most errors were eventually corrected, but the last two events—discovering the basement bathroom rough-in, and that same day finding they had cut three-quarters of the way through all the two by four's in a wall of the upstairs family room just seemed crazy.

For some unlikely reason, instead of being angry, this time we began to laugh. How could anything else go wrong?

We loved this beautiful golf course community and personally knew two couples who had already built there with no problems. But, that wasn't the case for us. Why had this seemed so right but had gone so wrong? It had taken great patience to get to this point, but that day neither of us felt like going forward without hearing something more from God.

I prayed:

> *Lord, this seemed like what we were supposed to be doing. Should we finish building this house or not?*

Heaven was quiet. The question was heavy on my heart; and after persistence on my part, finally an answer came. However, it wasn't what I wanted to hear. It was only one sentence: *"Go where the peace is."* That was it! "Go where the peace is." To tell you the truth I was a little ticked off. And maybe with a sassier attitude than I should have had, I quipped,

> *Lord, what's wrong with just telling us yes or no?*

We were up against a deadline and when heaven seemed to have nothing more to say on the subject, Paul and I began to explore where the peace was. After a couple of days, we agreed that the "peace" would be in letting the house go.

We made an appointment with the construction company's district manager, a fiery energetic little guy who reminded me of a bantam rooster—if you know what they're like, and he met us at the house. After pointing out each of the latest and greatest defects, his answer to each was the same. With a wave of his hand he would proclaim, "We'll fix it." Before long we could tell his intention was to try to promise us enough that we would stay in the contract. However, the day before God had given me what I felt was a perfect example to use for our meeting.

"Let me ask you this," I began, "Suppose you bought a really nice pair of two hundred dollar jeans and you found they had a huge flaw so you took them back to the store. They wouldn't give you your money back or replace them, but said they would put a big patch on them for you and your jeans would be as good as new. Just put several hundred thousand dollars on that example and you've got this house." With that, he conceded and agreed we didn't need to move forward any further. However, there was one big thorn left for us to deal with. They would keep $5,000.00 of our money.

Being rid of the house was a relief and there truly was peace in the decision, but I had another big question for the Lord: If that seemed so right to begin with, why had it gone so wrong, and why had we lost $5,000.00 in the deal? My heart went up to the Lord with this query on a regular basis. I truly wanted an answer. Was the inner voice I was hearing at times really Him, or was I just fooling myself? I began questioning my ability to hear the Lord and it seemed Paul was doing the same.

Quite a few months passed with no answer. Late one night I saw an ad in the newspaper saying this same builder was giving a cash incentive to purchasers on several houses in the development. After discussing it the next morning, Paul and I decided to go see Karen, their sales lady who we were well acquainted with after all that had transpired. Even though it had turned out to be a bad situation, we knew it wasn't her fault and our relationship with her hadn't been damaged. She was excited to see us.

We found out one of the homes they were advertising was bigger than our original. It was actually the floor plan we liked the best but didn't feel we could afford—a two story with vaulted ceilings and a beautiful spiral staircase among other grand features. It was on a prime lot next to the green area—a lot that had been under contract long before we started looking. But now the deal had fallen through twice when neither couple qualified for their loan. The builder was anxious to get it sold. They were giving a $40,000.00 discount to a new buyer. We were instantly interested, and in a moment of boldness we asked Karen to find out if they would give us our $5,000.00 back toward the purchase of the house. We were thrilled to hear they agreed to do it.

When all the figures were put together, the cost ended up being nearly the same as we would have paid for the other house. The difference in what we gained in the new house compared to the original was astounding. We were reminded what the scripture says in Ephesians 3:20–21:

> Now unto him that is able to do exceeding abundantly above all that we ask or think, according to the power that worketh in us, Unto him be glory in the church by Christ Jesus throughout all ages.

Those verses lit up.

Recently I read this statement in Mark Batterson's book *Draw the Circle* telling of his own house delay. I felt it spoke to our situation perfectly. "God often takes things away to give them back so that we know they are gifts to be stewarded for His glory."[1]

Once we knew the end from the beginning and looked in the rearview mirror, there was absolutely no doubt that our home was a gift from God and for His glory. It was a wonderful, beautiful, amazingly arranged gift; a blessing to us and all who entered through its doors and ultimately all we had to do was trust Him and "go where the peace was."

## Chapter Seventeen

# THE BIG SURPRISE!

A S I STEPPED through the door of the room we'd been assigned, I was startled. There she stood. It was Donna. I hadn't seen her for years.

This event had started so innocently. "Would you like to go to the writer's conference with me?" my friend Judy invited. Though we didn't live in the same city any longer, we were both interested in writing and it was an excellent opportunity to learn and also get caught up on each other's lives. I accepted her invitation.

The May air was crisp when I arrived at the beautiful setting in the Colorado mountains. After checking in I proceeded to our quarters. Judy had asked if it was alright if we shared a room with two ladies from a town near her to cut down on expenses, and I agreed. But as I stood there facing Donna—speechless for a second that seemed far longer, old memories flooded into my mind.

Back then rumors were flying: "She's having an affair. She is planning to leave her husband," and various other accusations. I had heard the rumors but I didn't have a very close connection to her, and I had no idea if the reports were accurate, and spent no time dwelling on them. But, suddenly there was a new twist, and it was all focused on me. I was told by those we knew in common she was accusing me of starting the stories. I believed there had to be some misunderstanding. Someone, surely, had gotten things mixed up. Soon it became clear there was no mistake. I was the one being blamed.

It was a crush to my tender twenty-something heart, and I felt hurt and angry. It would have been one thing if I was guilty, but I wasn't. What was I supposed to do? An appointment to see our pastor seemed appropriate. With tears of anguish I explained the situation to him. To defend myself seemed reasonable—to tell everyone who knew us both that I wasn't guilty and place the responsibility where it belonged.

His counsel was wise though difficult. "If you don't put any wood on the fire, it will go out," he challenged. At that moment it didn't seem fair, but I valued his advice and decided to do just as he recommended. With the help of the Lord, I dropped the issue—to let the fire go out. However, after a period of time we learned the ugly rumors had been true. Donna experienced a nasty divorce and married the other man.

Now there we stood facing each other in the room at the conference. For a moment I wondered how this was going to work out. Up until that point there hadn't been the need to dig deep within to see what was going on in my soul with this very old wound. As I quickly searched my heart, it was a relief to find that there was not an ounce of bitterness or unforgiveness left over from the past and I greeted her warmly. She was friendly in return and we continued through the conference as though nothing had ever happened between us.

Late on the second day, Donna came to the room filled with excitement. She had talked to an editor who thought one of her articles was worthy of publishing. We were all thrilled for her.

"Donna, can we see your article?" I proposed. She was hesitant, but handed it to me. As I read, it was something I hadn't anticipated. The story told of her journey toward forgiveness for the man who molested her granddaughter. As we soberly passed the pages among us, Donna began to cry. She related to us the horror of the situation and the sorrow and pain it had brought to their family. Trying to be the strong one for all involved had taken its toll. As we listened to her agony, in one accord the compassion of God welled up within the three of us and with a corporate anointing we began to minister to her with prayer and encouragement. She received it gladly. God had prepared the way for help and comfort to come to one of His hurting children.

It was almost time to leave. Judy, Donna, and I were standing outside the conference center saying our good-byes. Just then Judy remembered she had ordered some tapes and hadn't picked them up. As she left to retrieve them, Donna and I were alone for the first time. "I'm sorry for what I did to you all those years ago," she confessed. "Would you please forgive me?"

Her apology took me by surprise. But, thankfully, without hesitation I was able to say, "Donna, I already have."

Until I looked back I didn't understand how important forgiveness in that particular situation had been—forgiveness that didn't require an apology. There was no way I could have known that forgiveness would allow me to be one of those who ministered to a badly hurting child of God all those many years later—ministry that possibly could not have taken place had I harbored bad feelings in my heart.

And looking in the rearview mirror, our pastor's counsel for that incident has been of value—counsel that came straight from the Word of God. In Proverbs 26:20 it says:

> Where no wood is, there the fire goeth out: so where there is no talebearer, the strife ceaseth.

Over the years I cannot count the times I have made the choice not to throw wood on the fire.

## Chapter Eighteen

# GIVING A GOOD POUNDING

HAVE YOU EVER beat your *words* on the ground? Well, figuratively I have. It all started after an amazing blessing from the Lord, followed by a great big brand-new problem.

After a couple of years of struggle over the construction and purchase of a new house, God provided well above what we could have imagined. But, the new problem was this: after closing on our beautiful miracle home, our old house didn't sell. To add to the drama, Paul took a temporary position teaching air traffic control in Oklahoma. At one point we had an old house and a new house in Longmont, Colorado, and an apartment in Oklahoma City. After Paul's temporary teaching assignment was completed, though it had not been on the market the whole time, a year had passed since we had put our old house up for sale. Upon our return to Longmont, we became *very* serious about asking the Lord's help with the situation.

One day while in prayer, a Bible story came to me. I remembered the essence of it, but honestly, I couldn't recall where it was, or the names of the prophet and king involved. I looked it up and found it in 2 Kings 13. The king was Jehoash and the prophet was Elisha. Here's what verses 18 and 19 say:

> Then he [Elisha] said, "Take the arrows," and the king took them. Elisha told him, "Strike the ground." He struck it three times and stopped. The man of God was angry with him and said, "You should have struck the ground five or six times; then you would have defeated Aram and completely destroyed it. But now you will defeat it only three times.
>
> —2 KINGS 13:18–19, NIV

You may be thinking at this point, "What in the world does this have to do with selling a house?" Well, from that story I was impressed to think of my words as those arrows and figuratively strike the ground with them.

This is the phrase I felt the Lord gave me: though 10,000 houses in Longmont do not sell, our house is sold.

I didn't want to be like King Jehoash and do it half-heartedly and not receive the full victory, so I went about it with a vengeance. In the privacy of our home and when I was alone driving, I spoke those words with force though while driving I did get a few odd looks. I spoke them over and over with gusto.

"Though 10,000 houses in Longmont do not sell, our house is sold!"

"Though 10,000 houses in Longmont do not sell, our house is sold!"

"Though 10,000 houses in Longmont do not sell, our house is sold!"

Within three weeks we had a contract on our house.

You may be saying, "That sounds bizarre, and how do you know your house wouldn't have sold right then anyway?"

The answer is, I don't. But, I believe the enemy of our souls would like us to think when God answers it is some quirky coincidence or a mere happenstance.

During the time period when we wanted to sell our home, the housing market in Colorado wasn't good. I don't recall what we had been saying about selling our house, but through the story in 2 Kings, God definitely got our words in line with what needed to happen.

I began to realize—more than ever before—how our world is full of "word" pollution. Negative unproductive words bang into our ears from every direction like a 24/7 jackhammer. Sometimes they come from our very own mouths. With the help of the Holy Spirit, I determined to become a well-equipped sentry alert and watchful of every word that escaped from my lips, remembering that "death and life are in the power of the tongue" (Prov. 18:21).

Matthew 15:11 adds this: "It's not what goes into your mouth that defiles you; you are defiled by the words that come out of your mouth" (NLT).

When I look in the rearview mirror, I see that God was using the story in 2 Kings not only to help us sell the house but also to learn a truth that has been invaluable since.

*Lord, help me keep my words pure before you,*
*and also help me to never forget.*

## Chapter Nineteen

## DEGREES OF BLESSING

How is this making you feel?" Paul's brother, Ken, asked me. We were sitting in the stands waiting for the graduation ceremony to begin. Paul was receiving his bachelor of science degree from the University of Northern Colorado.

"I'm proud of Paul," I answered, "but actually, to tell you the truth, I'm a little jealous." With those words a twinge of guilt pricked me.

After less than a year of college, Paul had joined the air force. Now with a full time job as an air traffic controller, a wife, and two children, an opportunity to finish his degree had developed. The ATC facility where Paul worked had made arrangements with UNC in Greeley. There were enough employees interested that it became a reality. Most of the time the professors would travel to Longmont and hold classes at the ATC facility. It took several years and hadn't been easy, but Paul had done it; and I was grateful for his tenacity and strong work ethic that kept him going.

But as we sat there in the stands at graduation that day, I was reminded that my desire for a degree had not only been put on the back burner, it no longer seemed feasible. Present responsibilities, time, and money were not on my side.

Paul and I had met while I was attending Grace University in Omaha. I had only managed two semesters in two separate years—working and saving in between. We were married shortly after I finished the second semester. As time went by, life happened but college didn't.

In the next few years after Paul received his BS from UNC, God was gracious to allow me to accumulate a few college credits associated with my real estate career and also educational classes that were connected to being a tax professional, but still no degree. It was barely a thought in the back of my mind any more.

When one of our associate pastors at Resurrection Fellowship announced we would begin a unique Bible college called Christian Life School of Theology (CLST) at our church, we didn't take much notice. However, as information began to spread and the excitement of the students and their learning experiences became known, it got our attention. Monthly, besides receiving a text book for each class, professors were flown from all over the United States to our campus for intensive instruction over a three-day period. Often the professors were renown in the subject they taught, and it seemed like an opportunity of a lifetime. When we learned CLST was offering bachelor, master, and doctorate degrees, our interest was perked even further.

All this transpired in the year Paul decided to retire from his air traffic control position in Longmont. The timing was perfect and we began CLST classes. Paul's degree gave him a head start; but, thankfully, I also received advanced standing for my few college credits and the extensive tax related educational classes I had accumulated. In a time shorter than I envisioned, my lifelong dream came true and we walked into the auditorium to the sound of "Pomp and Circumstance" to receive our bachelor of theology degrees.

The classes were so enriching and such a blessing that we continued our education. I was even given the opportunity to work for our local campus under the exceptional leadership of our dean and assistant dean, Randy and Judy Mirowski. And like God does so often going above what we can imagine, after several years with hard work and diligence, once again Paul and I, dressed in cap and gown, marched to the sound of graduation music to each receive our doctor of ministry degree.

When I look in the rearview mirror, I see the resurrection of a dream that had become nearly dead being brought to life in our own backyard. And with that resurrection came a wealth of knowledge, information, wisdom, and inspiration from God's Word that will live with me forever. And what a blessing to share it all with Paul.

*Lord, thank You for bringing dead things to life.*
*I'm so grateful nothing is impossible with You.*

Hope deferred makes the heart sick, but a dream fulfilled is a tree of life.
—Proverbs 13:12, NLT

## ⁓ Chapter Twenty ⁓

## BACK TO THE FUTURE

UDDENLY PAUL FOUND himself floating near the ceiling of our large church sanctuary. Looking down he could see the entire congregation as they sang. As head usher he had gone to the rear of the building to observe and make sure all his ushers were in place. When he realized he was near the acoustic tiles above, he wondered if he had just died and felt for his pulse. His heart was beating.

He didn't hear a voice, but in that moment an impression came: "It's time to go back to Oklahoma City."

*"Okay, Lord,"* he surrendered, and immediately he returned to his body below.

As we drove home from church that morning, I had no reason to disbelieve what he was telling me. He wasn't one to embrace that sort of thing when someone made their claims and was sometimes the one to pooh-pooh the whole deal (just like some of you may be doing right now). I knew he wasn't lying or joking. And when he told me what the impression had been, I wasn't surprised. God had already been working on my heart.

The pressure for Paul to teach air traffic control for the University of Oklahoma in Oklahoma City had been there for quite some time. It wasn't until we discovered he could accept a few short-term assignments that would enhance our retirement situation that he considered it. The temporary positions had been a welcome diversion over a three-year period. But our goal had been accomplished; and though they wanted him to stay, Paul told them with a smile, "The best thing about Oklahoma will be seeing it in my rearview mirror as I head home to Colorado."

But that morning in church he had gotten a new directive. When he called the ATC academy in Oklahoma, they were thrilled. They wanted him to return immediately, but there were ends to tie up. Among other things, we were just finishing our last classes with Christian Life School of Theology (CLST) to each receive our doctorate and we had a house to sell. It was our beautiful miracle home. When we moved in, God had already impressed upon me our stay would be short-lived. Because of that I hadn't gotten tremendously attached.

Though possibly with only as much faith as one grain of mustard seed—or a half a grain—I told the Lord it would be so ideal if we could close on the house and move the weekend *after* CLST graduation in May. That way we would still have a place for those who came for graduation to stay. And although at times it seemed impossible, that's exactly how it happened.

We managed to secure a short term rental agreement on a house in Oklahoma City in a subdivision we had already spotted—where each of the homes backed up to one of several small lakes. From the patio of our rental, we could see the yard of the place across that lake that became our own home a few months later.

Meanwhile, Paul went back to the routine of teaching. It wasn't long before he was assigned the job of training a group of potential air traffic controllers from Puerto

Rico. The percent of those passing the difficult training was generally small, and there was no reason to believe the new class would be any different. One day Maria came to Paul's office. She had observed the Bible on his desk and asked, "Are you a Christian?" After he answered in the affirmative, she added, "I'm a Christian, too. Would you pray for me?"

Paul knew the decision to become an air traffic controller had been difficult for Maria. The opportunity came shortly after the birth of her first baby whom she had left in the care of her husband and mother. Not only were the classes demanding, but she was very homesick. However, this job meant a tremendous amount to the welfare of her family and she desperately wanted to succeed. Paul prayed for her that day; and after he told me, I prayed for her, too.

Some of the class members began to pray together, and since it seemed to be helping it spread among them. "Is it alright if we come to your church?" Maria asked a few weeks later. As we met them at the door of the church Sunday morning, nearly everyone in the class was present.

Victory Church had been a lighthouse to us each time we had been to Oklahoma City on temporary assignment. Our pastor was especially gifted in evangelism, and that day was no exception. The Spirit was there to draw people into God's kingdom. When the invitation was given for those who would like to take Jesus as their Savior and Lord, nearly the whole group responded. Tears of joy and amazement blurred our eyes as we watched them file to the front and make their commitment.

Classes weren't over, and becoming a Christian was not a guarantee of success. Paul knew there was no room for leniency in their training because lives would be at stake. However, there was no doubt they were an outstanding group. Prayer was working on their behalf. The percent of those who passed was well above the average. And the success continued. A note of thanks received from Maria after returning home was good news. All who had succeeded in Oklahoma had also passed their final training in Puerto Rico. She and the rest had officially become air traffic controllers.

As we look in the rearview mirror, we can see many reasons why God directed us back to Oklahoma. But one of the things that stands out is the class from Puerto Rico. And as those students look in their rearview mirror, they would probably say they had no idea they were coming to the United States not only for training, but also to have an encounter with God.

*Thank You, Lord, for letting us be part of it.*

# Chapter Twenty-One

# GOOD GRIEF, LADY!

I DON'T KNOW WHAT'S wrong with me, Judy," I lamented. We had obeyed the directive from the Lord to return to Oklahoma, and we knew it was exactly what we were supposed to be doing. But all too often I was filled with a feeling of sadness and unexplained tears.

God had prepared so many things ahead of us; I was disgusted with my feelings. Even though I told myself, "Straighten up! You have nothing to be sad about," it did no good.

Paul's job was going well. The kids and grandkids were all fine. Our church was great. We had purchased a beautiful little home on a lake, had moved in, and were settled. And God had even supplied great new friends and reunited us with a few we had met earlier.

We were back with Pastor Mary Lou. Almost everyone called her Mama Lou. She had picked us out of a crowd of thousands the first time we stepped through the door of the church and made us feel welcome. Older than some of the seniors she shepherded, her energy level was that of someone half her age.

Mellodee and Jerry were also friends from one of our temporary assignments. We had met at VIP's, Mama Lou's group for those over fifty. The first time I saw

Mellodee I wanted to get to know her, and I was not disappointed. Beautiful inside and out, she and Jerry were also kind and generous.

And almost immediately after arriving, we were invited to join a small group of couples who gathered for game night once a month. We enjoyed their friendship immensely, not only on game night but any time we could get together.

So what in the world did I have to be sad about? It certainly wasn't because we were lonely.

I wasn't planning on whining to Judy. It just came out. She and I had already been prayer partners for several years. We had started our prayer time when I was working for Christian Life School of Theology (CLST), and she and Randy were the dean and assistant dean. In the beginning our prayer focus had been for the school; but it had grown to include, among other things, our government and family, as well as our own personal needs. I was grateful our new phone plan allowed us to continue our weekly prayer time long distance at no extra cost.

"Let me pray for you," Judy offered, and she began. I don't recall everything she said, but I do know, as usual, it was potent. But these words I remember: "I come against a spirit of grief." Right then the words pricked my heart.

"That's it, Judy," I responded when she finished, "It's grief." I still didn't understand it, but there was a partial release in my soul immediately. I still had a question: With all that was going so right, why would a spirit of grief have a hold on me? The answer wasn't long in coming.

That night as I told Paul about my conversation with Judy, he surprised me. He had been going through similar feelings. However, God was bringing us both to the same revelation in a very different fashion.

Paul had begun reading the book *Man of Valor* by Richard Exley. When he came to the part about Richard and his wife, Brenda, leaving their secure and familiar pastorate of twelve years, Paul read this:

> Although I grieved for months, I never once regretted my decision. Most major life changes are initially experienced as loss followed by a period of grieving that is both normal and appropriate. Grief is a healing emotion providing closure, while regret is an unhealthy fixation on the past life.[1]

The light turned on for us. We were both grieving; and Paul felt like he was also regretting, not the decision to obey the Lord, but he equated it with the children of Israel wanting to go back to Egypt. He still missed his home state of Colorado—the state where he was born and raised and where he had lived almost his entire life. We had left "all things familiar" when we moved: precious family, wonderful friends, thirty-seven years in the same city, twenty-one years at the same church, the beautiful mountains out our windows, and everything else we were accustomed to.

We learned it was normal to grieve but not to stay in grief. We still had work to do, but it made sense when we finally understood what was happening. We purposed to grieve appropriately for our loss, and move on— and I was able to do it without much delay. But for Paul, it was a longer process. He was out of Colorado, but he had to get Colorado out of him.

When we look in the rearview mirror, we are grateful for the revelation we received about our emotions back then. God was so faithful to bring us what we needed when we needed it. Not only did it give us peace and comfort as we continued our lives in Oklahoma, but it was a huge help the next time we left "all things familiar."

## Chapter Twenty-Two

# WELCOME HOME

L OOKING PAST THE clutter, we viewed the space. The renters were moving and every cupboard had been emptied on to the counters ready for the packers. We already knew one part of the property measured up—the three-car garage. It was one thing we had asked for. Even through the clutter, we could see the *only* rental of its kind available in Lubbock, Texas, at that time would certainly fulfill our needs.

We were taking a step of faith as we anticipated leaving Oklahoma City for Lubbock in West Texas. Our plan had been to go back to Colorado, but we began to think God had a different idea. To be closer to our grandchildren and their parents who live in Carlsbad, New Mexico, would be great; and it seemed that possibly God was fulfilling that desire.

It hadn't been an easy transition. Not wanting to live right in Carlsbad, we still hoped to be able to see our son and his family more frequently and to shorten the eight-and-a-half-hour drive from Oklahoma and even longer drive from where we had lived in Colorado. However, when Paul's job ended in Oklahoma City, the housing crisis had begun. Though the problems weren't severe in Oklahoma, the constant barrage of "house" news at the national level scared sellers and seemed to make buyers think they could purchase a home for practically nothing. We didn't feel it was necessary to sell at a loss.

As we waited for a contract on our beautiful little home on a lake, I questioned God.

*Is moving to Lubbock what you really want us to do? If it isn't, just tell us. We will go where you want.*

Each time I searched deep in my soul, it always led back to the same place—Lubbock; and Paul was experiencing his own personal journey in that direction.

Lubbock hadn't even been on our radar screen until we began driving through it on our way to Carlsbad from Oklahoma City. Gradually we took notice. There was Texas Tech University, a huge medical center, and an airport servicing several airlines, as well as plenty of shopping and eating establishments. We knew we wanted to be in a place where Pamela, our flight attendant daughter, could visit easily; and this place qualified.

But there was one more very important thing that needed to be checked out: the churches. If we couldn't find one to both receive from the Lord and serve Him, we knew it wouldn't be the city for us. Our online search began, and we visited services in several churches at times when we drove through on our way to Carlsbad. Our spirits were attracted to Church on the Rock, and we felt it was a place where we could worship. The city had passed the final test.

There was a certain dread of starting over again. We had already experienced that five years earlier, and it wasn't easy.

Finally, after two years that seemed like an eternity, our house in Oklahoma City was under contract and about to close. And in God's never-ending ability to time things perfectly, the non-typical rental I spoke of earlier became empty the day before we moved to town. We learned it had been constructed as the personal residence for the builder, but because of divorce it had become a rental. It had great amenities and though its sea-green carpet and the huge multicolored flowers on the wallpaper didn't match a thing we owned, it didn't matter. It had everything we needed—and more—to keep us comfortable until we decided on the home we would purchase.

We had already been looking at houses months before we moved and found nothing of satisfaction. At that time we were determined not to settle for one that was just "okay," but to believe God for the home that would be everything we desired. Construction companies became our focus. We noticed homes of one particular builder that really appealed to us. When we saw the company truck out front at one of his houses, we stopped. It was actually closing day for the new owners and they were moving in. Obtaining permission to look around, we loved what we observed. However, a few days later when we contacted the builder he informed us he had signed a contract the day before with someone else and wouldn't be able to work with us for a year. Since his homes were so beautiful and we had no clue about contractors in town, we requested his recommendations, and he mentioned several. But then he added. "If I were you, I'd contact Dan Wilson. He is the best builder in town."

A few days later our appointment at Dan Wilson Homes went exceptionally well. Somewhat apprehensive after our building experience in Longmont, Dan put our minds at ease and we signed a contract. On the day of groundbreaking, we met Dan and several of his family members and workers at our lot, took pictures digging the first spade of dirt, and circled for prayer. It was a great start. Soon we were going ahead full steam. Rod, the superintendent for our home, was an experienced builder who was knowledgeable and accommodating and the framing crew was excellent. (And I choose to believe the pizza and doughnuts we brought them on a fairly regular basis had nothing to do with it.) Carla, their decorator, was an ever-present help with the many material and color selections. I won't say that a problem never arose. There were some. But I can honestly say that each was eliminated in a timely and satisfactory manner. After ten months in Lubbock, we moved into our new house.

Besides the one-of-a-kind rental and our beautiful home, God has given us numerous opportunities here in Lubbock. We have many new friends, a great church where we can worship and serve, and a closer proximity to our children and grandchildren. And, it has been a joy to watch the grandchildren grow.

Once more God went before us and prepared the way, reminding me of the following scripture:

> We can make our plans, but the LORD determines our steps,
>
> —PROVERBS 16:9, NLT

*God, thankfully You don't have a rearview mirror. You can see it all from beginning to end. You are the Alpha and Omega. You have it all figured out ahead of time—and I'm glad.*

## Chapter Twenty-Three

# LET THE
# DECORATING BEGIN

SOMETIMES GOD'S ATTENTION to the smallest things in life amazes me—things that seem to have no eternal value and if you didn't pay attention could be missed entirely. Over the years when I look in the rearview mirror I see them as what I've heard referred to as a "God wink." I believe it gives God pleasure when we recognize the little things He does for us. So it was with the desk.

When we knew we would be leaving Oklahoma, I decided to replace my really big, really heavy corner computer desk with a lighter one that would be easier to move. After selling the large desk, we headed to Mathis Brothers Furniture and found just what I had in mind—on sale of course. It was a Hooker brand cherry wood with sleek lines, a black inlaid top, and a pullout keyboard drawer with a small drawer on each side. It was perfect.

When we finally moved into our new home in Lubbock, there was room for Paul to have a desk, too. Not that I'm the world's greatest decorator—or even close, but I did want his desk to look compatible with mine and, if possible, to match. I searched the web as well as most of the furniture stores in town and came up with nothing.

We even considered picking one up in Oklahoma City when we went to visit friends, but Mathis Brothers no longer carried them. Some of you search experts may be saying, "Well, if you would have done *this* or done *that* you would have found it." I'm telling you I did all I could think of and couldn't come up with anything suitable.

As always I had been talking to the Lord about it. I don't get angry with Him when He doesn't respond as if He is my errand boy, or my genie in a lamp; but I do talk to Him about almost everything.

About the time I had given up, my eyes fell on an advertisement in the Sunday newspaper. There in the Dillard's ad—of all places (I didn't even know they sold furniture) was my exact desk right here in Lubbock. And, of course, it was on sale. One more time God was showing me His sweet love. I could almost see Him winking in the rearview mirror.

## Chapter Twenty-Four

# Rx: The Best

W E SAT THERE in the examining room sensing the young doctor's disinterest and listening to his vague comments. As we left and made our way down the hallway to the receptionist's desk, we were surprised by what we heard.

"That's not what the doctor told us," one of us announced.

"Well, that's what he just sent me on the computer," was his reply.

Not knowing how things could get that mixed up in less than three minutes, Paul and I gave each other a questioning look as we made our escape.

After having a great general practitioner in Dr. Hinman and then his son for over thirty-seven years in Longmont, our move to Oklahoma had brought minimal exposure to doctors. But as we settled in our new home in Lubbock, we started to search for permanent replacements for those we had left behind. What we found had taken us by surprise and was a little disheartening. We were unhappy to learn when Medicare became our primary carrier and the good insurance we had kept from Paul's working years was our supplement, the cost of insurance for us went up significantly but it paid much less for our care than before.

For the first time in years we were no longer prime patients, and our search for a new doctor wasn't as easy as we thought it would be. Asking friends about their recommendations, we contacted several practices only to be told either they weren't taking new patients or they didn't take Medicare. Thus we had ended up in the office of Dr. Space Cadet who was, in fact, willing to take us on. Not only had he seemed to care very little about anything we told him, his communication to us and then something different to the receptionist was a little scary. We definitely would not be visiting him again.

At that point I realized I hadn't made it a matter of prayer. After asking God to forgive me, I petitioned Him to direct us to the right place.

A short time later as my beautician was cutting my hair, we were discussing her recent illness and started to talk about doctors. With that I began to bemoan our dilemma including the fact that Dr. Drylan at an office near us had come highly recommended, but he wasn't taking new patients.

"I see Dr. Parker at that same place, "she divulged. "He is fairly new and he takes Medicare patients."

Since it seemed a good thing to at least be in the same building with highly recommended physicians, I contacted their office and made appointments for us. As we interviewed Dr. Parker at our first meeting, it seemed the mild-mannered doctor was going to give us good care. And there was one detail of our interview that was highly unlikely. We found out he had practiced medicine for three years in a clinic in Longmont, Colorado, where we had lived for all that time. He even knew Dr. Hinman. It became a unique connection between us.

After about two years we received an unexpected letter from our physician. Dr. Parker was leaving. He had accepted a position with a corporation in another city. It was sad to lose him, but as I read the remainder of the letter I smiled. All of Dr. Parker's patients would be absorbed by the other physicians—and we could choose which one we wanted. And of course you know who we chose; the highly recommended Dr. Drylan.

Our trust is still in our God and His healing power, but we also know that Satan didn't invent doctors—well, most of them anyway. God uses them every day to help many, and He made a way for us to continue to have the best.

*Lord, I see You in the rearview mirror. Sometimes You make things happen in a most unusual way.*

## Chapter Twenty-Five

# ROOTS

L OOK WHAT I found in Grandma's trunk, "I announced. "It's a directory of the congregation from Cumberland Presbyterian Church dated March 1916. And guess where it's from."

I hadn't looked in Grandma Kemp's trunk for ages. Keeping her trunk and its contents hadn't seemed like any big deal until we started moving around. By now we had toted it from Colorado to Oklahoma and on to Lubbock in West Texas and sometimes we wondered why. But that morning when I opened it, the booklet right on top got my attention.

"Where?" Paul questioned as he took it from my hand.

There on the front in block letters it read "Lubbock, Texas."

Inside we found Grandma's uncle, W.R. Buchannan and his wife listed as part of the congregation. Of all the things Grandma saved in the trunk, we had no idea why she kept this particular item. However, suddenly it was of interest to us, because Lubbock had become our home.

Though we were aware of no direct ancestral connection to the city, this discovery sent me searching for the journal of our family tree from decades past. Grandma Kemp had gone to heaven more than forty years earlier, and I had no recollection of the information she had given me. But when I viewed her page in the journal I saw this: Moved to a farm near Lubbock, Texas, when she was eight.

Wow! Now we had a small connection with Lubbock. It was kinda neat.

A year or so later, Paul's distant cousin, Lowell, a serious ancestry buff contacted us. He and his wife, Ann, were traveling through Lubbock on their way to New Mexico and he wanted to go to the Lubbock cemetery to do some research. We agreed to meet him there. As we used his cemetery maps to navigate our way around, we came upon the graves of W.R. Buchanan and his wife—the ones in the 1916 directory. But what happened next was unexpected. There standing before us were the headstones of Paul's great-great grandparents, Albert and Ursala Buchannan. And before the morning was over we had discovered the headstones of Paul's great grandparents on the Kemp side, too. It gave us a strange and almost eerie feeling. Paul was a direct descendant of these couples, but he had no idea this is where they lived or where they were laid to rest. Had we been directed here for some type of unfinished family business?

*God, I see You in the rearview mirror; and though we didn't know it at the time, you brought Paul back to his roots. And I have a feeling that isn't the end of the story.*

## Chapter Twenty-Six

# THE BUCK STARTS HERE

E EACH OPENED the envelope we'd been handed and found a one-dollar bill. It was Easter morning, and our pastor explained this was seed from the church. We were to take it and multiply it for God's kingdom as we increased our vision for what God wanted to accomplish in the city of Lubbock. We were to bring a special offering at an appointed time several weeks away. The pastor made a couple of suggestions. One of them was to buy a cake mix and make cupcakes to sell. Since cooking isn't my greatest gifting, that didn't appeal to me in the least.

The dollar stayed in the envelope for a few days tucked away in my Bible. But the challenge had been unique, and one day as I was driving my thoughts went to the Lord about the dollar. What if I watched when Hobby Lobby had their beads at 50 percent off and made a bracelet to sell? But as I prayed, it seemed in a lightbulb moment the Holy Spirit gave me His idea. I was to go to Mardel Christian Book Store and buy a book for one dollar and offer it for more.

Mardel had been a favorite place of ours for years, and I knew they always had a large supply of books in their bargain area—many of them for a dollar each. So, off I went to begin the tedious job of searching through hundreds of books for the one I wanted to buy.

Much to my amazement I found more than one that appealed to me. There were authors I recognized and loved and even recent books. I asked Paul if I could invest his dollar, too, and he enthusiastically joined in on the challenge. I found so many that day I decided to loan myself ten dollars and start out with twelve books. Each one I purchased had a retail value between ten and twenty-five dollars.

As our "Books in a Bag" adventure progressed, we dragged them with us everywhere. Friends and family were happy to participate because with few exceptions they received an extraordinary bargain as well.

It seemed important to pay back the ten dollars right away so the original two-dollar seed from the church would stand on its own. Each time our inventory grew low, we headed to Mardel for a new supply. Like hasn't happened since, we found outstanding volumes from great authors that appealed to us and we felt would appeal to others.

When the Sunday came for the special offering, just from our two-dollar investment alone we were able to bring $200.00 to the Lord. And that's not all. We had forty books left in our bag that were donated to the library at the Dream Center, our campus on the other side of town.

I know it doesn't compare with Jesus feeding the five thousand with five loaves and two fish. But as we look in the rearview mirror, it makes us realize with His idea no seed is too small for the Lord to multiply.

## Chapter Twenty-Seven

# ALONE?

I FELT VERY ALONE, which wasn't really like me. It had been years since I had attended the Christian writer's conference in Colorado with my friend Judy. Now there I was again, totally on my own.

I had really wanted to go but had nearly talked myself out of it when Paul found on the Internet outrageously low priced plane tickets to Denver and we bought them on the spot. After that there was no turning back. And though Colorado was our old stomping ground, I wasn't aware of any acquaintance of mine who was going to the conference. It bothered me more than I thought it should. I'd confided in my Lubbock writing friend Cheryl, and she prayed a fervent prayer on my behalf—and I was grateful.

After arriving and checking in, I headed to my sleeping quarters hoping to meet my mystery roommate, but she hadn't arrived. I had prayed it would be someone who was compatible. Sometimes rooming with a person you don't know can be a challenge.

Still feeling alone with the crowd all around, I did my best to get my bearings as to where the teaching rooms were located and nervously began to set up appointments with editors I'd read about ahead of time—ones I thought might be interested in my material.

Mealtime came and I joined the long line of people waiting their turn in the cafeteria. A pretty blonde stepped in directly behind me, and we began to talk. Her name was Lucinda Stein, and she attended the same church in Grand Junction as Paul's brother's family. It was beginning to feel like a smaller world. She was at the conference alone, too, and we were happy to find each other. As the line began to snake around inside the building, I heard someone call my name; and there at last was a familiar face. It was my longtime tax client Colleen. I had prepared her and her husband's taxes for at least a decade, as well as tax returns for many of her family members. I hadn't seen her for at least ten years, and I had no idea she had an interest in writing. We hugged each other across the barrier and continued our places in line.

As we ate, Lucinda and I were getting acquainted. Among other things, I learned she is a published fiction writer. As we were finishing our meal, Colleen came to join us.

"Which building are you staying in?" I inquired.

"Mt. Ypsilon Lodge," she replied. It was good to hear that she was in the same building I had been assigned.

"What room are you in?" was my next question.

When she answered, I lifted my key and dangled it in front of her and she read the number. We had been assigned the same room.

My eyes got a little teary as I realized how thoroughly God had gone before me and prepared the way. No coincidence. God alone got the credit—the One who loves us with an everlasting love. As I looked in the rearview mirror I saw that He had made these arrangements weeks ahead of time—days before I would ever find out. He was surprising me.

Colleen and I had a great time catching up on our families as we lay in bed at night and soaking in all there was for us at the conference. Colleen, Lucinda, and I celebrated each other's progress along the way and encouraged one another during the day. The conference was a tremendous blessing, and I was grateful that God had arranged it so I couldn't back out.

Oh, and there was one more little indication of God's loving hand at work. Where was the room Lucinda had been assigned? Directly across the hall.

# Chapter Twenty-Eight

## A STROKE OF GENIUS

Y OUR DAD GOT home the same time I did," Cindy told their daughter Julie over the phone. "He staggered into the house and he isn't making any sense. I don't know what in the world is wrong with him. I'm taking him to the hospital. Can you meet us there?"

Challenging the speed limit as she drove from their home in Carroll, Nebraska, to Norfolk, Cindy answered a call from Julie. "Is he possibly having a stroke, Mom?" Julie questioned. Cindy had read an e-mail only days earlier about how to identify a stroke victim. One new test was fixed in her mind: Ask the person to stick out their tongue. Her request was met with only a blank look. Brad had failed the test and emergency room personnel were informed and ready. When Brad and Cindy arrived, the diagnosis was verified and the medical staff went into action.

One miracle had already occurred. If Brad had gotten home before Cindy and had lain down, she would have thought nothing about him taking a nap. But that day they arrived at the very same minute.

However, that miracle didn't mean there wouldn't be complications. Brad's employment for the last twenty-four years had been a truck driver—the tedious job of hauling factory-built homes to their destination in one of several states; oversized loads that took nerves of steel and an eagle's-eye alertness to maneuver. Now he was told because of the stroke he would lose his truck-driving license.

It wasn't that he would mind a different job. Especially since our nephew, Mike, died in a truck accident the year before. Since then there had been some night-mares. However, at that point another job was the least of their concerns. He was in the hospital having suffered a stroke, but because of their quick response the clot-busting drug had been administered with barely any time to spare. And much to the amazement of the doc-tors and medical staff, Brad walked out of the hospital in less than forty-eight hours completely and thoroughly recovered—no paralysis and no speech or mental inca-pacitation. Prayers had been answered.

But financially he needed to work, and who was going to hire a sixty-five-year-old truck driver who no longer had a license?

Wanting to do her part, Cindy saw an ad for a position working in food services at Wayne State College near them and decided to apply. Since driving of any kind was completely off limits for a period of time, to get out of the house Brad went along. Once there, he decided to fill out an application, too. What could it hurt? The hiring supervisor just *happened* to come by as they were completing the paper work.

"We're looking for a breakfast cook," she commented.

"Then he's your man," Cindy encouraged.

Though Cindy did most of the cooking at home, and a great job I might add, Brad loved to cook breakfast. He had spent many Saturday mornings preparing a grand meal for the family. Suddenly it all seemed to be coming together. Brad had a heart for young people and this appeared to be a God-given opportunity to be near a never-ending source of youth. He was excited when he called to tell me about it.

"Did she hire you?" I questioned.

"She said she'd get back to us," was his reply. But, for the next few days they heard nothing.

Driving privileges still restricted, Brad stayed the night with their son, Perry, and his wife, Leah. With Perry as his chauffeur, he was happy to join the men in his early morning Bible study group. With the job at Wayne State still in his heart, he asked them to pray. After the meeting Michael handed him a card with two names on it.

"Go see one of these men," he encouraged.

Brad read the names on the card and placed it in his wallet. Retrieving it a few days later, he told Cindy about the conversation. Turning it over for the first time he saw that it was actually Michael's business card. This is what it read:

Northeast Community College
Dr. Michael R. Chipps
President

Brad knew Michael worked for the college, but had no idea he was the college president. Arriving at the office of the food manager, one of President Chipps' recommended contacts, the manager wondered how they knew about the jobs he was yet to advertise. Showing him the card solved the mystery, and both Brad and Cindy were hired on the spot depending only on the required background check. It was the same type positions they had applied for at Wayne State and would have equal access to the students. Their desire to be in a place to minister to young people and speak the love of God into their lives had come to pass.

But, at *this* college there was a bonus. They were told money would still be coming in during time off in the summer and over the holidays—precious time off to spend with their own six children and many grandchildren.

Physically the job had its challenges, and the transition wasn't the easiest. But it was just a few short weeks until I heard some of the ways they had been ministering to the students—helping a young man from Africa learn English, taking international students for a day at the zoo, and welcoming others to their Thanksgiving table.

Sometimes God walks with us down a very strange path to get us where we're going. A stroke? *Really, Lord?* We would never have prayed for such a thing. But thankfully God can use for good what our enemy means for evil, and it led to a job change which came about in a way there was no doubt God was involved.

At times it is very interesting what we see God doing in our rearview mirror.

## Chapter Twenty-Nine

# In Conclusion

I<small>T WOULD BE</small> nice at this point if we could say we will all live happily ever after. But, as long as we are on this earth, that isn't going to happen. Jesus Himself said in both Matthew 18:7, and Luke 17:1 that offences *will* come. But we can take comfort in the knowledge that as we put our trust in Father God, Jesus our Lord and Savior, and the Holy Spirit; use the Bible as our training manual; and listen closely for His voice in our spirits; we can live a joyful, victorious, and peace filled life. And with God on our side, we *can* get through anything this world tries to hand us.

We may not always understand as we look forward; but just as you have read in this book, many times we can see God clearly in our rearview mirror.

## Now it's Your Turn

Your life may be completely different than mine, and your stories may or may not have a resemblance. However, from the smallest events in life all the way to actions, decisions, and answers to prayer that change our circumstances drastically or dramatically, we can know in our heart of hearts when God has been at work.

Now it is your turn.

If you have a story that is uplifting and encouraging and you recognize when you look in the rearview mirror that God was working on your behalf—let us know. We are accepting new stories to chronicle in a future volume of *God in the Rearview Mirror.*

Please send the essence of your narrative in fifty words or less to Godintherearviewmirror@gmail.com along with your name, address, e-mail, and phone number.

God is alive and well. Many times we can understand perfectly what He is doing. Other times we need to encourage each other to keep trusting God until we finally recognize Him smiling in our rearview mirror.

## GOD'S KINGDOM

If you happened upon this book but you have never asked Jesus to be your Savior, there are two scriptures that makes that choice understandable, simple, and clear:

> For God so loved the world, that he gave his only begotten Son, that whosoever believeth in him should not perish, but have everlasting life.
>
> —JOHN 3:16

> If you confess with your mouth that Jesus is Lord and believe in your heart that God raised him from the dead, you will be saved.
>
> —ROMANS 10:9, NIV

All you need to do is ask. Pray something like this:

> *Father God, I know You are missing in my life and I haven't served You. Please forgive me when I have failed. I believe Jesus came to save me from my sins, and I ask Him now to be*

*my Savior and Lord. Take my life and make it what You want it to be.*

There is no magic in the words. But if you meant them from your heart, God will honor your decision and give you His life.

When we give our lives to Jesus, it is just the beginning. As you grow in your knowledge of Him, may your new life with Christ bring you peace like you have never experienced before, love that didn't seem possible, and take you places you never dreamed achievable. May you see God clearly through your windshield of life, and may He regularly appear in your rearview mirror.

# NOTES

### CHAPTER SIXTEEN:
### A LEMON BECOMES LEMONADE

1. Mark Batterson, *Draw the Circle: The 40-Day Prayer Challenge* (Grand Rapids, MI: Zondervan, 2012).

### CHAPTER TWENTY-ONE:
### GOOD GRIEF, LADY!

1. Richard Exley, *Man of Valor: Every Man's Quest for a Life of Honor, Conviction, and Character* (Lakeland, FL: White Stone Books, 2005).

# ABOUT THE AUTHOR

LAVILA HENRY, ALONG with her husband, Paul, is a ministering elder at her home church and serves both locally and internationally as a teacher and intercessor. Her desire is to see pastors and church leaders come into the unity of the Spirit and pray with a new intensity, knowing God hears and answers.

Before retirement LaVila enjoyed careers both as a tax professional and a real estate broker. She and Paul have been married more than fifty years and have a daughter, son, daughter-in-law, and three beautiful grandchildren.

# CONTACT THE AUTHOR

*Email:*
Godintherearviewmirror@gmail.com